DATE DUE

RETIRED — Enjoy This Book!

THE MIRACLE OF JIMMY CARTER

THE MIRACLE OF JIMMY CARTER

by Howard Norton
& Bob Slosser

Logos International
Plainfield, New Jersey

First edition—June 25, 1976

The Miracle of Jimmy Carter
Copyright © 1976 by Logos International
All rights reserved
Printed in the United States of America
International Standard Book Number: 0-88270-202-5
Library of Congress Catalog Card Number: 76-20393
Logos International, Plainfield, N.J. 07061

to Marjorie and Gloria,
our wives

CONTENTS

Acknowledgments

We want to express our gratitude to all the people who made this book possible, especially to every person at Logos International, whose prayers and hard work wrought miracles. We owe a special debt of thanks to Jessie Gover, *National Courier* news assistant, who toiled so arduously and patiently over the preparation of the manuscript.

And we are grateful for the kindness and help of the candidate himself; his wife, Rosalynn; his mother, "Miz Lillian;" his sister, Ruth Stapleton; his brother, Billy; his cousin, Hugh; his uncle, Alton Carter; his old friend, Mrs. Clarence Dodson; City Manager, W.C. Lamb Jr., and all the good people of the marvelous little town of Plains, Georgia, such as Glossie Howard, Ernest Turner, and Maxine Reese.

And we thank and congratulate all members of the Carter campaign organization.

Howard Norton
Bob Slosser

PROLOGUE:
Suddenly It Was Over

When this year is over, the political textbooks and the history books will have to be rewritten. Things are happening that haven't happened for more than a hundred years; other things are happening that have never happened before. There is a sense of history in the making; a feeling that something mysterious and irresistible is at work behind the scenes.

The purpose of this book is not to try to explain away this sudden and unexpected turn in American politics, but rather to shed light on the man at the center of it all, the former governor of Georgia, Jimmy Carter, and on his spiritual life and his temporal background, which seem to have worked together to bring him to this moment in history.

A hint of what is happening in the political year 1976 can be seen in outline in the long and growing list of political "firsts" that we are witnessing with Carter:

The first presidential nominee from the Deep South since before the Civil War.

The first presidential nominee within memory to reach that party pinnacle without help from the party leaders, and without owing political debts to anyone.

The first presidential candidate to take with him to his party's national convention such a high total of primary-won delegates—the highest on record.

The first presidential nomination that was won, for all practical purposes, before the primary election season was half over.

The first presidential candidate to start so low (four percent of his party's voters) and soar so high, so fast.

The most primary-election votes ever cast for any candidate in either party.

First in the largest number of votes in the primaries, 6,162,809 (fourteen percent of the total registered Democrats in the U.S.).

The first presidential nominee in history to confess openly to the voters that Jesus Christ came first in his life.

The first presidential candidate to be hailed by the political polls as a "sure winner" by a wide margin over the incumbent president while the primaries were still under way and months before he got the nomination.

There is more, but that should be enough to show why so many people look upon this year and this election as one that could bring a spiritual revival to the United States and its government.

When the 1976 primary elections came to an end on June 8, Carter was officially credited with about 1,200 delegates, 300 short of the number needed. But the opposition had collapsed. Within twenty-four hours he had all the delegates he needed—and more. The stop-Carter movement had vanished. Governor George C. Wallace and Senator Henry M. Jackson had urged their delegates to vote for him. Mayor Richard J. Daley of Chicago had pledged support. Senator Hubert H. Humphrey had once again withdrawn from a race that he really never got around to starting. Nomination was assured.

Washington, D.C.
June 9, 1976

1

FAITH:
THE DIFFERENCE

My religion is as natural to me as breathing.

– Jimmy Carter

A veteran newspaper reporter, first-hand witness to half the presidential campaigns of this century, sat down to write about Jimmy Carter. He wanted to show "what makes Jimmy run." It would be easy. He could do it in an hour. There would be plenty of time, afterward, to take the dog for a walk before dinner. No problem, the facts were all clear.

"Ambition is the key to the character of Jimmy Carter," he wrote. "This man wants to be president. He wants it more than anything else in this world. In fact, he wants nothing else in this world. And he'll do anything that needs to be done, and say anything that needs to be said in order to achieve that ambition . . . ."

He paused a moment, and read what he had written. He shook his head, ripped the paper out of the typewriter and put in a clean sheet. He had remembered, suddenly, some-

1

thing that had been said by one of the Carter campaign aides who sat beside him as the candidate and the accompanying press flew between stops. He began, again:

"Jimmy Carter is just plain stubborn. He's too stubborn to admit that the odds are heavily against him. He's so stubborn, in fact, that he may just become our next vice president. For even Carter-type stubbornness is not enough to convince the voters that this country is ready for a Deep South president—especially one from Georgia. . . . And then there are the smoke-filled rooms at the convention. Is Carter stubborn enough to intimidate the old professional party leaders? . . .

Again, the words stopped flowing.

"Reads all right," he thought. "Might even be true. Newspaper readers have short memories. If it comes out that way, I can remind them I said it. If it doesn't, no harm done. . . ."

But somewhere in the deeper recesses of his journalistic conscience a warning bell sounded. It happens all the time to professional writers and interpreters of the news. A lifetime at the job packs the memory bank so full of incidents and facts and unwritten stories that even the most experienced reporter has trouble sorting them out and producing them at the exact moment they are needed.

Then it came to him, like a sharp, tingling electric shock.

"Faith!" he said aloud. "That's it! He has faith! The kind of faith it takes to move mount . . . no, not to move mountains—that's for Reagan and his Panama Canal problems. This man Carter has got the kind of faith that moves voters—millions of them." Ambition he's got, yes. And he *is* stubborn. But those are not the basic elements. Jimmy Carter has faith—faith in the Lord Jesus Christ, faith therefore in himself, and faith in the American people. And the voters can see it. It may not be so clear through the haze of the smoke-filled rooms inhabited by the political bigwigs.

Then the reporter's memory-bank moved into high gear. "Faith!" It was so obvious! How could he have missed it? There was that time in 1975, almost before the campaign had gotten underway. Friends and neighbors in Carter's native Plains, Georgia, population 683, had proudly hoisted a banner to the top of a store building on the block-long Main Street: "Home of Jimmy Carter—Our Next President."

Jimmy thought it was a nice gesture, and he said so. But, privately, it looked to him more like a danger signal.

At that time he didn't have a single delegate to his name; in fact, not even a single vote. The primaries were still months away. But candidate Carter looked at that sign through his mind's eye—and with faith in his future—as he would see it from behind the desk in the Oval Office at the White House.

What he saw gave him a start.

Sandwiched in among the two grocery stores, the two filling stations, the hardware store and the antique shop that make up the Plains business district, he saw a honky-tonk array of cheap souvenir shops, selling made-in-Japan souvenirs of President Carter to crowds of eager tourists.

While this vision was still clear, the former governor of Georgia set about to protect and preserve his beloved hometown from the side effects of his own future success. He asked for new zoning laws and legal restrictions. He told friends and neighbors that he did not want, as president, to ruin the little Georgia town they all loved—the home of five generations of Carters, the calm oasis where candidate Carter went almost every week to rebuild his strength from his roots in the red Georgia soil.

The town of Plains, he said, will be even more important to him after he is elected. "Keep it like it is," he pleaded. "This is my place for prayer and meditation. Here, in the quiet Georgia countryside, I can think. I need this place."

This kind of faith—a faith that leads to planning far ahead for things he is convinced are certain to come—was characteristic of the Carter campaign for president. It explained a lot of its success.

For example: Almost a year before he became an active candidate, the ex-governor and his friends began filming campaign television commercials. By the time the first of

Carter's opponents began to think of putting together commercials for television, a Philadelphia company had already
shot more than five miles of film about Carter, and had some
commercials ready to go. Then, before the April Pennsylvania breakthrough—his first convincing victory in a northern industrial state—the same Carter group was already
putting together a twenty-minute film to be shown on
closed-circuit television in the delegates' hotel rooms at the
New York convention in July.

This, remember, was at a time when Senator Hubert
Humphrey had quietly entered the stage door and was
standing in the wings. It was a time when the wiser heads of
the Democratic party were spreading word that Carter
couldn't make it; when conventional wisdom was that he
would emerge from the smoke-filled rooms as no more than
the vice-presidential nominee.

But in the elation of election night in Philadelphia it leaked
out that the Carter camp's TV department was even further
ahead of the political game than anybody had guessed.

It was putting together at that moment a grand finale—a
TV special to be flashed on a giant screen behind the
speaker's rostrum *the night that Governor Carter accepts the
nomination.*

Now *that* is faith. Faith, in an important way, is self-
fulfilling. It gave the Carter camp the confidence to move
ahead, while others, more timid and less confident, waited
for the verdict of the voters, and fell behind. So, when
victory came, the Carter people were ready for it.

In another case, the Carter campaign ran out of money
just as the drive for Pennsylvania started. So the question
arose: Can we go in; can we get enough money together to
make it worthwhile?

The pundits were saying Carter just might win the "popu-
larity contest" but no way would he get many Pennsylvania
delegates. Senator Henry M. Jackson of Washington, heavily backed by labor, was certain to take the lion's share of the
delegate races, they said.

Candidate Carter brushed aside the doomsayers and met

the Pennsylvania financial crisis in two ways: He convinced the plane-leasing agency to loan him an aircraft for the campaign (the money he would receive from the reporters and Secret Service agents for their places on the plane guaranteed that payment would be forthcoming). And for the other expenses of the Pennsylvania campaign, he dipped into his own personal resources.

Obviously, faith again paid off. After the victory, money began to pour in.

Jimmy Carter's faith in himself was the target of more verbal nonsense in the media than any other facet of the campaign. They wrote that he had "enormous certitude," whatever that means.

"I don't pretend to know all the answers," he often said when he talked to small groups of voters. "I'm just like you. I'm not any more able or intelligent than any of you. But I feel you are talking to the next president."

He told them he "will never lie" to the American people. The media, apparently, interpreted this as the biggest lie he could possibly tell. To the cynics of the press, an honest man is as unlikely to be found as the Holy Grail.

For the first eight primary elections, faith in Jimmy Carter was the commodity he was selling to the voters. He was frankly fuzzy at times on many of the major issues. He admitted this. He told questioners he would solve those problems when he got into the Oval Office and got hold of the facts. No other candidate in this century campaigned that way. He convinced the voters that lack of experience in Washington was, in effect, an asset. It meant, he said, that he had no ties to special interests, that he didn't owe anything to anyone, and that he could bring a fresh approach to the individual problems that those close to federal affairs might assume to be natural and incurable.

"Have faith in me," he was saying in essence. "I am a Christian. I am an educated man—a nuclear scientist, a naval academy graduate, a naval veteran of eleven years, a successful businessman, the father of an attractive family, with no 'problem' children. I was a successful governor of

Georgia for four years. I believe in keeping government simple—and economical. If you like the way things are going in Washington, don't vote for me, because I'm going to turn the executive branch of government upside down."

In short, he was telling the voters that he was the kind of man most Americans would like to be; the kind of man they would like to have as their president.

They laughed, in New Hampshire, when somebody asked him whether he was a liberal or a conservative, or a moderate, and he answered: "I don't have to choose, so I won't."

As a matter of fact, reporters who covered his campaign knew that he was all three. And Carter himself said he saw no reason why any man had to be a radical on anything; why a man could not take a liberal stance in some areas, moderate in others and conservative in still others. That's the way most human beings are made up, anyway, he concluded.

From his public utterances it can be determined that Carter is sincerely liberal in matters of race, both moderate and conservative in the field of social legislation, and staunchly conservative in fiscal matters.

According to his wife, Rosalynn, it was his intense feeling against the waste of money in Washington, in fact, that first gave him an interest in running for president. He said, for example, that he thought he could give the country a stronger defense establishment for less than President Ford was spending. Defense was one area where he was an admitted expert.

He declared that within a year after he got into the White House, "there will be no more food stamps." He regarded the food stamp program—fathered largely by Hubert Humphrey—as one of the worst sources of government waste and one of the worst objects of massive thievery in the history of the country. He promised to see that the poor and the elderly were cared for, but under a completely new welfare system, not by food stamps.

As one who was not a part of the "mess" in Washington, Carter said, he would have a freer hand to clean it up. All of his major opponents, he noted, had Washington ties and

Washington records that they were likely to defend even if they reached the Oval Office.

Carter's refusal to define his political coloration, his refusal to make promises, had the usual effect of any double negative—the end result was positive.

Carter, experts said, sensed the mood of America better than anyone in either party. This carried him to the nomination.

Still he made no promises. He offered honesty, morality, frugality and Christianity in the Oval Office, to a country where "wealth accumulates and men decay." He asked only that the nation have faith—in itself, in its government, in its president, and in God.

Month after month, there was a feeling that something mysterious and irresistible was at work behind the rise of Jimmy Carter. You didn't sense it merely in the campaign rallies. There was, of course, excitement at those affairs, the excitement of discovery of something new in politics—a man who was comfortable with God. But it was when you stood off and contemplated the whole chain of events that you got the feeling there was more to it than met the eye or made the newspapers.

The smiling, friendly, virtually unknown man from Plains, Georgia, had little to smile about in January of 1976. On the twenty-second of that month the Gallup poll showed that he was the presidential choice of only four percent of the Democratic voters.

Yet, one month later, he won the New Hampshire primary. And within another thirty days, by the twenty-third of March, he had defeated George Wallace in Florida and swept through North Carolina, winning fifty-three percent of the total Democratic vote in that state.

Then, by the 27th of April, only three months and five days after that dismal "four percent" appraisal of his chances by Gallup, Jimmy Carter had virtually cleared the field of all effective opponents by winning in Pennsylvania, a state that is not only a northern and industrial state, but also labor-dominated and boss-ridden.

The statistics testify that there has never been another presidential campaign to compare with Carter's in enthusiasm and power. No other presidential candidate in either party won so many primary elections or so many primary-elected delegates.

What about John F. Kennedy? The man with the exciting charisma in 1960 won only ten out of the sixteen primaries, collecting a popular vote of only 1,847,259 Democrats. Carter won twelve out of the first fifteen primaries held this year; in those first fifteen primaries he got 3,872,976 votes, or well over double the number of votes cast for JFK in all of his sixteen primaries in 1960.

And in 1972? Senator George McGovern won only eight primaries, in all. The total vote cast for him in all of that year's primary elections was 4,053,451—about 9.6 percent of all registered Democrats in the country. With sixteen primaries still ahead, Carter was only 180,000 votes short of McGovern's final total and 8.6 percent of all registered Democrats in the country had voted for him. Less than halfway through the primary gauntlet, the Carter campaign thus began to set new presidential campaign records.

But even more notable, in the eyes of the old pro politicians was the absence of serious mistakes. The plans that were followed were the plans laid four years before. There were no mistakes serious enough to require major changes. Everything seemed to work. And this simply does not happen, not in any ordinary campaign, presidential or not.

Even the famous "ethnic purity" remark, in which he opposed the forced breakup of neighborhoods, contending that they should be allowed to retain their ethnic character, turned out to be a plus, not a minus. It may have been a slip of the tongue that brought forth those particular words. But the fact that they were spoken and the furor they aroused kept Carter on the front pages and in the television and radio spotlights during a time when it was important to keep his momentum going.

Faith: The Difference

According to the newspaper, television, and magazine pundits, Carter's miracle campaign was the result of great good luck and the diligent work of a handful of rank political amateurs. But luck and inexperience are not the stuff that miracles are made of.

Even in the early days of the campaign, many people said they sensed that the Baptist from Georgia might be moving under the direction of God himself. They didn't perceive Carter's rise to the forefront as the result of luck. Louis P. Sheldon, of Anaheim, California, a leader in the Full Gospel Business Men's Fellowship International, who observed Carter at close range, saw it this way: "God has his hand upon Jimmy Carter to run for president. Of course, he's wise enough not to be presumptuous with the will of God. But he's moving in the will of God."

Carter himself refused to fall into the trap set for him by reporters. He told them he didn't believe he had been "ordained to be president." Instead he said, "I've never asked God to make me president of the United States. I pray only that God will help me to do the right thing."

It seemed pretty clear to most observers before the campaign was very old that Carter was, indeed, doing the right things. The Carter camp took a poll of one Cleveland precinct made up largely of Roman Catholic blue collar workers of Czech and Polish extraction. More than half of those questioned said they would vote for Carter. Their reasons for the choice: his "honesty," "morals," "religion," and "character."

A thirty-one-year-old machine operator cited "sin and crime" as the main issues, and said he would vote for Carter because he was an "honest man."

The wife of a machinist said Carter's morals and character "seem to be better than any of the others."

A factory worker's wife picked Carter because of "highly moral standards and a Christian attitude."

A thirty-three-year-old waitress who said she was disappointed that Carter had not come out against busing, added that she would vote for him anyway because she was sure

9

"he'll do the right thing."

It seemed clear to all who understood such things that the miracle of Jimmy Carter was not based on luck. There was only one answer to that often-repeated question, "Who is Jimmy Carter?" The answer: "A man with faith in God."

As Carter traveled through the country, from state to state, making it clear by actions, and by words, that he was a Christian, millions of Christians rallied to his banner. Little data was provided by the pollsters to show what proportion of those supporting the Georgian did so because of his religion. It is believed there are about forty million evangelical Christians in the country, and that many of them were attracted by Carter's open profession of his faith.

In fact, Jimmy Carter was one of the best things to happen to American evangelical Christianity in this century. In the months that he was in the national spotlight campaigning for the nomination, the secular press did more to spread the gospel—by factual reporting of the Carter campaign—than all the religious press combined. Cynical, hardened political reporters by the scores learned what it meant to be "saved" or "born again," hardly standard-brand newspaper jargon. And, as accurately as could be expected under the circumstances, they wrote about it. To them, it was something new—it was news.

When Carter first appeared on the presidential scene, one noted reporter wrote: "Mr. Carter may well do for the Protestants what John F. Kennedy did for the Catholics."

His point was that Kennedy proved a Roman Catholic could be elected president of the United States; Governor Carter was trying to prove an evangelical Protestant from the Deep South also could make it to the White House.

But there was little further parallel between the two candidates in their manner of campaigning. Only once in the 1960 presidential campaign did Kennedy so much as mention his religion—at a meeting of clergymen in Dallas, Texas. It was common knowledge, of course, that he was a

Roman Catholic, but it didn't seem polite, at the time, to talk about it. So nobody did.

This was in sharp contrast to the campaigning custom of Carter. His faith was the item given top prominence when he began to get attention because he talked so openly and easily about it. "My religion is as natural to me as breathing," he said.

No other candidate since Al Smith, in 1928, has brought religion into the picture. And for both Smith and JFK, their Catholicism was regarded at the time as a handicap. Times have changed. For Carter, religious enthusiasm and an open confession and practice of faith turned out to be assets.

Carter does not claim to be a "strict" evangelical. He classifies himself, rather, as a "common-sense" evangelical, acknowledging that there's always something to disagree with in almost any given set of rules.

When he was governor, he outraged some of the Southern Baptist clergy by calling Georgia's ban on Sunday liquor sales "hypocritical" since many people patronized bootleggers on the Lord's day.

And one of his first acts, as governor, was to end what he regarded as the "pompous" religious service that Lester Maddox, his predecessor as governor, held in the state house every morning.

The prime source of Carter's faith is, of course, the Bible which he reads often and regularly for inspiration and guidance.

Carter is an avid reader, whipping through three and four books a week. He has spent a lot of time in the works of prominent theologians and philosophers, including Reinhold Niebuhr, Karl Barth, Paul Tillich, and Soren Kierkegaard, and he sometimes quotes them in his speeches. One of his favorite quotations during the campaign was from Niebuhr: "The sad duty of politics is to establish justice in a sinful world."

Some of the Democratic nominee's critics worried that his Christian life was so pervasive that it might improperly intrude on his actions as president. But, like the late President Kennedy, Carter denied any conflict between the two in his personal philosophy and promised a strict separation of church and state.

To those who questioned him he replied: 'Render unto Caesar the things that are Caesar's and unto God the things that are God's.' It does not say you have to live two lives. It doesn't say you have to be two people."

He insisted that, on the contrary, his beliefs would make him a better president. And in that goldfish bowl called the White House, there is ample opportunity for that to show.

2

IN THE BEGINNING . . .

I go to church on Sunday, but I don't think all churchgoers are Christians. I think there's a difference between religion and Christianity.

—*Mrs. Lillian Carter*

When you drive southeastward from the airport at Columbus, Georgia, you pass through mile after mile of forest, much of it native Georgia pine. There are farms, but not many. Most of them are small and they are scattered, and many of them show clearly the earmarks of poverty.

After about thirty minutes of this, still in the forests, you begin to climb. A roadside sign notes "Americus 20." And as you reach the top of a hill there is a quick glimpse of the road ahead—a rolling ribbon that looks like the back of some prehistoric monster serpent. So for the next ten or fifteen minutes it's up and down, up to the summit and then a swift ride down into a valley, and then another climb.

Suddenly, just as you begin to get used to the rhythm of climb and descent, it ends. Your car labors up to the summit of a final hill and there, stretching out to the horizon—as level as the top of billiard table and just about as green—are broad, vast and beautifully cultivated fields of farmland, the peanut-growing plains of west-central Georgia, Just ahead a neat, white sign announces that you are about to enter the town of Plains, Pop. 683. So now you know where the town gets its name.

Reporters who have descended like locusts on this hometown of Jimmy Carter have, for the most part, fixed their minds on politics and ignored the scenery. They have given the country a picture of Plains as a dusty little place, built around a block-long business district of dilapidated buildings. Nothing could be further from the truth.

The town of Plains—the major part of it, the part where the people live—is a shady, restful oasis, with wide, smoothly paved streets and sidewalks that are shaded by tall, overhanging oaks. It is a town where large, well-kept white clapboard homes, dating back fifty to seventy-five years, far outnumber those of more modern dates and more modest size. It is a town of people who take pride in their homes, keep their lawns close-cut and their shrubbery trimmed. To the casual first-time visitor it looks like a good place to live, a good place to come home to, a good place to relax. It is easy to understand why Jimmy Carter flies so many hundreds of miles just to spend a few hours there, among family and friends.

True, the "business district" is not pretty, by any standard. And that's where the highway passes through, so that's about all travelers get to see.

Main Street is one block long. On one side there's a row of century-old red-brick store buildings, built wall-to-wall and in poor repair, awaiting the start of a "restoration" project that has been in the planning stage for five years. On the other side of the street are the Seaboard Railway tracks, now seldom used except by an occasional freight train. The old wooden depot, painted a glistening white, stands out as the centerpiece of the business area, the main tourist attraction and the center of about half the downtown activity. A sign posted on the east end of the depot and visible for one hundred yards down the highway reads, "Jimmy Carter

14

Campaign Headquarters." And at the top of the old and now unused railroad signal tower is another sign exhorting: "Jimmy Carter for President."

The town is tremendously proud of Jimmy. When it was decided to take over the dilapidated depot as the campaign offices, to handle Carter's personal mail and telephone calls, the whole town turned out to help with the renovation.

The first day they came with tools and materials to repair the leaky roof. Next they attacked the peeling outside walls with putty knives and gallons of paint, and then the inside walls and floors. And when the fixing and painting was done, they showed up again with their pickup trucks loaded with chairs, tables, desks, filing cabinets—even a television set. The century-old former Seaboard depot is now the prettiest building in the whole business district, outshining even the brand-new one-story modernistic building that houses the Plains branch of the Citizens Bank of Americus—the only modern building in the business block of Main Street. It sits just diagonally across the street from the depot.

The Carter name is everywhere. At one end of Main Street, the corner of Main and Bond, is the low, flat-roofed office building for the Carter Warehouse operation, the family firm now being managed by Billy Carter, Jimmy's thirty-nine-year-old brother. A few steps up Main Street, Jimmy's cousin, State Senator Hugh Carter, has offices for the Carter Worm Farm, "the biggest one in the world," according to Billy. And the last two of the business buildings, at the opposite end of Main Street from the Carter Warehouse building, have been combined to house the wholesale and retail antique business run by Jimmy's eighty-seven-year-old "Uncle Buddy" (Alton Carter) and his son, Senator Hugh. And in between is a busy hardware store owned by a former Carter business partner, Ernest Turner. From every window in the block a "Carter for President" poster smiles out at passers-by.

The townspeople have only one regret about the things they can do for Jimmy: They'll never be able to post a memorial plaque on the house where he was born on Oct. 1,

1924. The house, owned by Emmett Cook, who died in May, 1976, was being rented by the Earl Carter family at the time. It stood right across the street from the Plains Methodist Church. But it was torn down some years ago to be replaced by a modern home.

Life was less pleasant and considerably less prosperous for the town of Plains and for the Carter family when Jimmy was a barefoot boy. But, looking back, Carter said he realized that he had led a contented and happy childhood, despite the grinding poverty of the time.

His earliest recollections centered around a clapboard farmhouse in the hamlet of Archery, about three miles from Plains—a house without plumbing, lighted by kerosene lamps, heated by fireplaces and wood stoves; a house cool in the summer and cold in the winter. "But I never had any overwhelming fears or deprivations," Carter said. "My life has been singularly free of really traumatic experiences. I lived a sheltered life. My mom and my daddy were always there when anything went wrong in the fields or in the woods or in school. Home was always a haven. So I never had any fears. There were no villains in my life, that I can think of."

There were only two white families and twenty-five to thirty black families living in Archery at the time. Carter's playmates were black; his schoolmates were white. But there was not much time for play. Even as a pre-school child Jimmy was sent into the fields with a hoe and a "poison mop" to keep the boll weevils off the cotton. And if he needed or wanted money, he was encouraged to earn it. His cousin, now State Senator Hugh, recalled the ways they used to make their spending money in this isolated farming community:

"We used to take our little red wagons and go around to the houses and collect newspapers, and we'd sell them to the stores to wrap mullet fish in. And we'd haul scrap iron. We got twenty cents a hundred for it. We'd go to the city dump to find pieces, and we'd go around to the houses, too, and collect bits of iron. And then we'd sell it to an old fellow here.

"When we were in high school we used to sell ice cream, three dips for a nickel. Our mothers made it for us, and we'd color it red, no matter what it was, and we'd sell it out here on the sidewalks when the farmers came to town on Saturdays. And we'd sell hot dogs for a nickel apiece, and boiled peanuts, five cents for a big bag."

It was the day he graduated from high school that Jimmy showed the first real sign that he was, indeed, his father's son. Graduating at the top of his class he was awarded a scholarship to Georgia Southwestern College in Americus. As recalled by Mrs. Clarence Dodson, a close family friend, this is what happened:

"Jimmy was at the head of his class, and the girl who came second in scholarship was Eloise (Teenie) Ratliff, who came from a large family, with several sisters and only one brother. Her parents could not send her away to college. So Jimmy took the scholarship and turned it over to Teenie, and that's how she went to college."

Mrs. Dodson also recalled that Jimmy's father, Earl Carter, saw to it every year that all the girls in the Plains high school graduating class had the long white dresses they used to wear at graduation in those days. Girls too poor to buy the dresses were given their dresses anonymously by the elder Carter.

"When Jimmy came back home after his father's death," Mrs. Dodson added, "he continued to provide graduation dresses for the needy girls until they changed over to wearing caps and gowns."

Jimmy's younger sister, now Ruth Stapleton, a well-known Christian with a nationwide healing ministry, said: "I don't think we will ever understand his ability to work harder and longer than any other candidate—or why the Secret Service calls him 'Dasher'—unless you consider the physical and emotional training he had from his earliest childhood. I'm certain that a major influence on Jimmy's positive emotional development was his father."

When Earl Carter ran for his first public office, a seat in

the Georgia House of Representatives, only about twenty votes were cast against him in all of Sumter County, which was his district. Those twenty votes, according to Mrs. Stapleton, came from one family—his competitors in the peanut business.

When Earl died, the reasons for this exceptionally high esteem among the voters were made known to his family for the first time in a flood of notes, letters and visits from people of the community, both black and white. Some who said that they had been unable to buy or rent land for farming, had been given plots to farm for their living by Carter. Others told the family that their meager incomes had been supplemented by Carter trust funds, established by "Mr. Earl." There were notes from students whose whole college careers had been underwritten by him. In all of these cases Earl Carter had insisted to the recipients that his benevolence be kept secret. Until his death, no one, even in his own family, knew anything about these matters.

"But we did know there was depth in him which demanded respect," Mrs. Stapleton said. "The point I'm trying to make," she added, "is that Jimmy's deep will to serve the public and his integrity seem quite unbelievable, and deserving of cynicism until you see the model for his manhood—his father. His honesty and strength are not a part of a public relations pitch. He received them through a rare relationship with a truly good man."

Mrs. Stapleton said it was this revelation of his father's commitment to the community and its people, and not business considerations, that led Jimmy to terminate his naval career and devote himself to a life of public service. Carter himself confirmed this in a recent interview.

"My father had terminal cancer, and I had to go home to be with him for the last month of his life," he recalled. This was in 1953, at a time when Carter was head of a team developing a new nuclear submarine, a job he considered one of the best in the navy.

"I guess I always had wanted ultimately to be chief of Naval Operations." he continued. "But when I went back home to where I had lived, and when I saw what my father's life had meant in the view of those who knew him best, his service on the school board, his work for the new hospital, his dealing with the education of farmers, his life in the church, and his life in politics—he had just been elected to the legislature and had served one year when he died—I could feel a pull on me that was almost irresistible to go back and renew my ties to my birthplace.

"I felt I had to make the choice. Did I want to be chief of Naval Operations, and devote my whole life to that narrowly defined career, which was a good one, or did I want to go back and build a more diverse life with a lot of friends, and have permanent stability in a community, an integral part in the life of a·whole group of people? And I chose the latter.

"Regrets? None at all."

Carter's roots in the Plains area of Georgia are deep—200 years deep. The first members of the Scotch-Irish Carter clan arrived there in the late 1700's and Carters have lived there ever since. The main body of the family never moved away.

The family was always "cash-poor" because it used its money to acquire land. Jimmy Carter and his immediate family now own or control about 4,000 acres near Plains. That's six and one-quarter square miles. About two thousand of those acres are said to be owned by Jimmy himself; peanuts have always been the cash crop.

But the late father of the Carter family, Earl, also ran a store and started a warehouse business where he sold seeds and other items to surrounding farmers. Jimmy, and now his younger brother, Billy, have built the warehouse venture into a business that grosses two and one-half million dollars a year. Thus, even while he was off politicking, or serving as governor of Georgia, Jimmy drew an income of forty to fifty thousand dollars a year from the family enterprises.

Governor Carter said he felt his lifelong habit of prayer had kept him on the right path. "I've never regretted a day I served in the navy," he said. "That was an opportunity for me that paid off. It gave me a chance to travel extensively. I read, and studied, everything: music, art, drama, and so forth. I stretched my mind, and had a great challenge and I never had any regret for a single day that I spent in the navy. And I never regretted getting out of the navy after I left."

Carter spoke warmly of his father, but described him as a stern man, who was not to be disobeyed and who expected to be addressed as "sir" by his sons. "I never disobeyed my father," he said, and then explained that he meant he had never disobeyed when his father said, "Jimmy, you do something." He always said, "Yes, sir," and he did it.

"But, of course," he added, "on many occasions I did things that I knew my father didn't like, and I was punished very severely because of it."

His mother told of one time he did something his father didn't like.

"We gave him a penny to take to Sunday school when he was very young," she recalled. "And when he got home and was changing his clothes we found he had brought *two* pennies home. Well, my husband took him by the hand and took him right back to the church and made him return the extra penny and hand over the penny that he failed to put into the collection. That was worse than any spanking, for Jimmy."

Carter recalled that his father very seldom gave a direct order. "If all the other field workers were off for the afternoon, and he wanted me to turn the potato vines so he could plow on Monday, daddy would say to me 'Hot' (he called me Hot-Shot), 'would you like to turn the potato vines this afternoon?' And I would much rather have gone to the movies or something, but I always said 'Yes, sir, daddy!' And I would do it. But he didn't have to give me many direct orders, and I never did disobey a direct order."

Carter insisted that his obedience to his father was not a namby-pamby sort of thing. "My father was a friend, and I respected him," he said.

Jimmy Carter was the first person in his family to finish high school. To go to college was, in itself, a notable goal to reach in the Carter family at that time, the candidate said.

He studied hard and finished high school at the top of his class, he recalled, because of a driving desire to go to the naval academy at Annapolis where tuition was free and which, therefore, offered him his best chance to get a college education.

But, by the time Jimmy got out of high school, the financial pinch was so much reduced that he went right into college while still waiting and still determined to go to Annapolis. For the 1941-42 school year he was a student at Georgia Southwestern, and in 1942-43 at Georgia Tech. Then the big break came; Annapolis was opened to him. He graduated in the class of 1947 and was commissioned an ensign. By 1953, when he resigned from the navy, he had risen in rank to lieutenant, the equivalent of a captain in the army.

Jimmy Carter credits two women with a major influence on the molding of his character in his early life. One of them, "Miz Julia" Coleman, was the superintendent of his school when he was growing up in Plains. The other was his mother, now a peppery seventy-eight-year-old, known to the whole town as "Miz Lillian."

"I'm much more like my mother than I am my father," Carter said. "She is a reader. She reads day and night. At the breakfast table, lunch table, supper table. I did, too. She encouraged it. And I still do. My father didn't read much. He read the newspaper and maybe *U.S. News & World Report*, and that was just about it.

"Mother was always a champion of disadvantaged people. She took all the poor regardless of color, under her motherly wing. She was a registered nurse, and later, when she was sixty-eight years old, she joined the Peace Corps and went to India to use her training, as she could, to help the disadvantaged there. She's always been that way."

"Miz Lillian" held a lengthy and lively conversation near the end of the presidential primary season, in the restful living room of her "pond house" tucked away under a forest of pine about two miles out of Plains. Just outside the big picture windows, lively, fattening bass were jumping at low-flying bugs in an acre-size spring-fed pond as she talked of her son and her daughter-in-law Rosalynn and other members of her family.

"I think one of the reasons Jimmy is so successful is that he reads books," she said. "He reads every kind of book. I never did censor what he could read. I'm that kind of a mother.

"When people want to know what makes Jimmy tick, what influence I had on my children, I tell them it was just a day-by-day influence. But I did tell my children one thing: Always do what you think is right, and don't pay any attention to criticism."

She was asked: "Are you as religious as Jimmy and Ruth?" Fixing the questioner with a direct gaze, "Miz Lillian" said, "No, I'm not."

"Someone else asked me that once," she added, "and it was printed somewhere, and I got a letter from somebody who said, 'Oh, I'm so sorry you are not a Christian.' Now that's not the idea.

"I'm a Christian, the way I see it. But I do a lot of things the ladies of the church think I shouldn't do. I smoke when I want to. I take a drink late in the evening; I used to do it with my husband before he died, and I still do. I'm allergic to tranquilizers; I'm allergic to everything except my little drink of bourbon. But there are just so many things that I do that long-faced, dyed-in-the-wool Christians do not do.

"I don't have the faith that Ruth does. I don't understand her book, *The Gift of Inner Healing*, like I should. Jimmy and Ruth, they both love me, and they think of me as being a Christian. But they never try to foist their deep religion on me. I think Jimmy loves me more than anybody else in the world except his wife. And that's right."

"Miz Lillian" paused a moment in this frank discussion and then went on:

"I tell you, here's a good way to sum it up. I go to church on Sunday, but I don't think all churchgoers are Christians. I think there's a difference between religion and Christianity.

"My kindness to the underdogs in Georgia has always

been criticized by people. But, thank goodness, I can go to bed at night and go to sleep thinking: 'I haven't done anybody any wrong.' How can people who say they are Christians be so cruel?

"During Jimmy's governor's race, I'm sure I was good for him. I'm one of his best public-relations people.

"There's not a person around here, black or white, who doesn't know me and how I feel about them. Believe me, Jimmy is going to get all their votes. The folks here love Jimmy and they trust him.

"I think I'm on the right side of God. I think he likes what I do."

"Miz Lillian" spoke warmly of daughter-in-law Rosalynn.

"I'm her mother-in-law and I love her dearly," she said. Then, with a twinkle in her eye, she told how Rosalynn had "caught" Jimmy for her husband.

"Rosalynn was Ruth's best friend, always," she explained. "And she was at my house almost every weekend, and when she wasn't with us Ruth would go into Plains and spend the weekend with Rosalynn.

"Well they were high schools girls, and Jimmy knew Rosalynn as one of Ruth's young friends, and he'd say, 'Hi, Rosalynn' when he came home from Annapolis on vacations, and that was it.

"Well one night Jimmy and some friends decided to give a dance with a jukebox over at the pond house, and Ruth and Rosalynn were with us that weekend, and he said, 'Why don't you get somebody to bring you and come and join the party.' So they did.

"So Jimmy danced first with Ruth and then with Rosalynn, and he asked Rosalynn, 'Don't you think the girl I brought is pretty?' And Rosalynn snapped right back, 'She's not half as pretty as I am.'

"And I think Jimmy noticed her then for the first time. And a few days later he came into the kitchen and said, 'Mother, do you know who I have a date with?' I said, 'Who?' and he said, 'Rosalynn.' And they began to date every night when he came home from school. And he never again dated anyone else. Rosalynn tells me she had a crush on Jimmy for two years before he got around to noticing her."

The other woman who Carter believes had significant influence on him as a child, the teacher, "Miz Julia" Coleman, saw in him "a hunger to learn," according to Jimmy. "She made sure that I listened to classical music. She made me do it. And she made sure that I learned about the famous paintings and artists.

"And she gave me a list of books to read, and she was very strict with me," he added. This gave him a strong taste for reading, he said, and it stayed with him.

It was rather a stern life, his childhood in Plains, Carter conceded, but "there wasn't much to do in our spare time anyway, if we'd have had more spare time, which we didn't."

"We didn't have any movies in Plains. I remember that when I was a very young child we had a small bowling alley that was not nearly as long as a regular one was, but it was an exciting thing for Plains when we had a bowling alley for a while—the kind with the small balls.

"But my life was spent out in the woods, and in the streams and swamps and fields."

Cousin Hugh had a bit more to say about Carter fun and games during a conversation in his Plains antique store.

"On Saturdays," he said, "we liked to hitchhike to Americus [about ten miles] and go to the movies. We didn't have automobiles. We would have had to ride bicycles, and that was a long bike-ride.

"Then we used to go find a sawdust pile—when a man had his timber cut, they'd cut it right on his land and leave a big sawdust pile. And we'd take the sawdust and find us a creek and dam it up and make us a swimming hole. And we'd just strip off our clothes and go swimming. Then, at night, we'd get out our cooking gear and cook a meal and spend the night out there, and go back home the next day.

"Jimmy liked to hunt. His daddy and my daddy would take us hunting early in the morning, and we'd shoot about sunrise. Jimmy got to be a pretty good shot, and he still likes to hunt. But he does it mostly on his own land, now."

Cousin Hugh was a candidate to take over Jimmy's seat in the Georgia State Senate in 1966, the year Carter lost his race for the governorship. He still holds that seat, and the folks around Plains for years have called him just plain "Senator Hugh."

It was to Senator Hugh that Carter first broke the news that he and his immediate family had decided he should run for the presidency. As the senator tells it:

"Jimmy came to my house, he came around and knocked on the back door, about two months before he announced for the presidency. He said, 'Hugh, I want to talk to you.' So we went into the den, and he said, 'I've got something to tell you, and I want all the family to know it first: I'm going to run for president of the United States.'

"I looked at him a little in awe, and I said, 'Jimmy, you mean that?' And he said, 'Yes I do.'

"Isn't it amazing how fast he has risen in this election?" Senator Hugh asked. And then he offered to explain why it had happened:

"One big reason is that Jimmy is a Christian. Our fathers took us to Sunday school since we were babies. We are all members of the Plains Baptist Church, and we believe in Christ, we love Christ. And if you are a Christian, it will show in your life, and it shows in Jimmy Carter's life. It shows in his sincerity, in his smile, in his frankness, in his courtesy to people.

"And when Jimmy Carter talks to you, it grabs you, right off. You can feel the sincerity in him. And before you know it, instead of him talking to you, he'll have you talking to him, telling him about your life.

"My advice to you is this: If you don't want to vote for Jimmy Carter, if you don't want to get out and work for him, then stay away from him. Because if he talks to you, you're going to be hooked!"

As the conversation drew to a close, Senator Hugh put in one more remark:

25

"He's going to win, you know. He's going to be president. And do you know why I know? Because he's talked to enough people in the last four years. When he's talked to them, they're hooked!"

Hugh, as clerk of the Plains Baptist Church, is keeper of the records. His books show that Jimmy Carter was baptized in 1935 at the age of eleven, after making a public confession of his faith in Christ.

He explained that the Southern Baptists do not christen or baptize children in infancy. "In the Baptist church," he said, "when you reach the age to know your mind and heart, you say publicly you have given your heart to Christ and then you are baptized."

Besides his father, the man having the most influence on Jimmy Carter's life was Admiral Hyman Rickover, the Jewish genius whom the navy once tried to scuttle, but who persevered against opposition and succeeded in creating America's fleet of powerful nuclear submarines.

Carter had applied for transfer to Rickover's nuclear program. He became one of the admiral's favorites—one of a group he called his "navy four,"—four who came into the program during the designing and construction of the submarines *Sea Wolf* and *Nautilus*, the first two built.

"Rickover demanded of me a standard of performance and a depth of commitment that I had never before realized I could achieve," Carter said.

Having spent more than six years in the navy, Carter said he realized there would be a suspicion that he was at heart a militarist and likely to favor the navy over other branches of the service as president and commander-in-chief.

"There's no aspect of militaristic inclination now on my part," he said. "I feel free of that, completely. But the discipline has stuck with me, and it has served me well. I have a constant drive to do the best I can. Sometimes it's disconcerting to other people, but it's not an unpleasant thing for me. I don't feel that I've *got* to win . . . or that I'd be terribly disappointed if I don't win. I feel a sense of equanimity about it. If I do my best, and if I lose, I won't have any regrets. But I feel that I must do my best. And that's what Admiral Rickover and the navy taught me."

In 1945, while Carter was still two years away from graduation from the naval academy, he and other midshipmen were taken on a North Atlantic training cruise.

It was on August 6, 1945, a calm sunny day, that the muffled, mechanical rumble of the ship under way was suddenly obliterated by the shrill piping over the loudspeakers. "Now hear this," a voice began. "This is the captain speaking. All hands will assemble immediately at the loudspeakers to hear an important announcement by the president of the United States."

This was followed by the sound of hurried movement and the jumbled, excited voices of men who had been expecting this announcement for days—the announcement, they thought, of the United States' invasion of Japan. As Carter himself related the incident, there was guessing about how many Americans would have to die to defeat Japan. About a half million seemed to be the consensus; no telling how many Japanese. So it was with mixed emotions—excitement mixed with a heavy sense of foreboding—that they waited to hear what the president was going to tell them.

When the president's words finally began to come through the ship's speaker system, when it came to them that it was not, after all, an invasion of Japan that he was announcing, but the dropping of a bomb of "unprecedented power" on the city of Hiroshima, there was confused silence.

"We had not ever heard a hint of anything like this," Carter said, relating the incident. "It was a mystery to us. We didn't, obviously, have any concept of what was going on. But I felt at the time a tremendous sense of relief that we had not, indeed, begun the invasion of Japan."

Carter said he now thought, with the advantage of hindsight, that President Truman had done the right thing. And he believed that he, as president of the United States, should he face a similar situation, would make the same kind of decision. He would choose, he said, the lesser of two evils: the Bomb, as opposed to the certain death of possibly half a million of his countrymen.

"I would use every resource in my life to prevent it," he said. "But I think I would have the capacity to make a choice between the lesser of two evils and, in my opinion, that was the kind of choice Truman had to make. So, in similar circumstances, my answer [on the Bomb] would be 'yes'."

Jimmy Carter is an attractive man. He seems to be a decent human being. But many Americans feel that his whole background has been provincial and mostly rural, that he is, by birth, a possibly narrow-minded man who has lived most of his life in the southern environment. The question they are asking each other is: "How can such a man seriously expect to lead a pluralistic American society, and the rest of the Western world as well?"

Almost exactly that question was asked of him in a television interview on a Public Broadcasting station with a limited viewer audience. He responded this way:

"I'm not sure that you have to have lived in many different places to understand a pluralistic society.

"I've had a changing career, myself, I started out as an isolated farm boy living, as a minority member, in a predominantly black neighborhood. I moved from that to a small town, and then from there to junior college, and from there to Georgia Tech, and then to Annapolis.

"I've traveled extensively in foreign countries all my adult life.

"In the last few years I've moved in foreign affairs, on the level with prime ministers and presidents, foreign ministers, defense chiefs, and so forth.

"As governor, for instance, when I've been in Israel I've been with Mrs. Meir and Mr. Rabin, and Mr. Allon . . . and Mr. Eban; when I've been in Japan I've been with Mr. Miki and Mr. Tanaka and Mr. Fukura and Mr. Ohira.

"So I've had a chance to learn, as a very eager student, the possible ways to improve our relations with those countries by talking with their leaders.

"I've read extensively, too. On the history of our country, the purpose of the presidency, the relationship between the president and Congress.

"I've studied every one of the 435 congressional districts in this country; their demographic make-up, their past voting records, the primary interests of the people who live there.

"I've studied the campaign platform of every person who's ever run for president—whether he won or lost.

"I've had a chance, as governor, to deal with a multiplicity of problems from different kinds of people; those who are mentally afflicted, those who are very rich, and want favors; those who are corporate giants, and want to preserve their privilege, those who are consumers and are hungry for a chance at the market place; those who are poor and illiterate, who are looking for justice and not finding it.

"In my own career-life, I was a farmer at first, and still am, now; I've been a businessman, in a business I built fairly much myself; I've been an engineer, a scientist, a naval officer, an official of local and state governments. . . .

"So I've had a broad background. That doesn't mean that I'm completely at home with all the elements of a pluralistic society. But I do believe my background to be the equivalent of that of many who have become president, and who have served successfully."

3

DEFEAT— AND NEW LIFE

*You've got to look beyond yourself
for God's purpose. You've got to
be less self-centered in all of your
life.*

—Ruth Carter Stapleton

One of the most significant periods in Jimmy Carter's
adult life followed right on the heels of deep disappointment,
failure, bitter defeat. It occurred at a time when the
world—business, social, political—seemed to be opening
wide for the well-educated former naval officer. He had
tasted the excitement of politics, responding to a strain
within him that apparently had flowed from his father, Earl,
and he showed evidence of unusual potential in that area of
American life.

At the age of thirty-eight, he had triumphed magnificently
in an ugly battle against ballot stuffing, a story of raw
political corruption of the worst kind on the local level, and
was elected to the Georgia senate. He began to learn southern politics—a politics all its own, especially before the
evolution of what came to be called the New South.

Then came an unusual series of events leading to what many would call the apex of Carter's development. First there was a decision to run for the United States House of Representatives against Howard (Bo) Callaway—a man who also would go on to figure more prominently on the national political scene.

Carter set a strong grass-roots campaign in motion. But then the leading Democratic candidate for governor suffered a heart attack, and Callaway announced his Republican candidacy for the governorship, apparently giving Democrat Carter a clear shot at Congress.

But then large numbers of young Democrats in his district, plus some fellow state senators and representatives of women's groups, pressured Jimmy to run for governor. Despite the temptations of apparent victory in the House race, the proposal aroused instincts within Carter—"not especially admirable," he conceded—to compete with Callaway. They had many points of rivalry, not the least of which was the fact that Callaway had graduated from West Point about the time Carter was completing his studies at Annapolis. And, obviously, they were both young Georgians on the move politically.

Following a procedure that was to be repeated over the next few years in other critical decisions, Carter first did a thorough job of brainstorming and analysis, and then turned to his most reliable confidante, his wife, Rosalynn. Together, they agreed he should run for the office of governor.

With only three months remaining until the statewide primary, Carter, his family, his friends, and his band of supporters in the district, opened a frantic campaign across the entire state. Prophetic of what was to happen nine years later, the biggest obstacle they encountered was typified by the phrase "Jimmy who?" He was virtually unknown outside his area, but his youthful team, again indicative of later efforts, mounted an all-out campaign that brought him, out of a million votes cast, just twenty thousand votes short of a place in the runoff. He finished third, behind former Governor Ellis Arnall and the segregationist restaurant owner, Lester Maddox. The latter, assisted by crossover voting by Republicans who figured Maddox would be easier for Callaway to beat, defeated Arnall for the nomination in the runoff.

Then in the general election, Callaway finished ahead of Maddox, but fell short of a majority. An old Georgia law, since changed, left it to the legislature to pick between the first two finishers if neither had a majority, and Maddox was chosen as governor.

"It was a great failure in my life," Carter said. "The entire experience was extremely disappointing to me."

Campaign debts were piled high. His health had suffered, resulting in a serious loss of weight. But, worst of all, Maddox, who stood adamantly for so many of the things that Carter abhorred, was governor for four years. And Carter was completely out of political office, having relinquished his state senate seat to make the race for representative and then governor. He and brother Billy returned full-scale to the business in Plains, sharing it as a family operation.

But Jimmy was still attracted to political life. Within one month, Jimmy disclosed plans to re-enter the gubernatorial race in four years. Working at his business in the early part of the day, he devoted the later hours to speech-making, meeting people, studying issues, writing letters, directing the activities of the strong band of young volunteers that was already gathering around him. Despite the time gap, it was full speed ahead.

"From 1966 through 1970," he said, "I worked with more concentration and commitment than ever before in my life."

But all was not well inside Jimmy Carter. The outer man was driving, scrambling, on the go. The inner man ached. "I began to realize," he said, "that when I had successes I had no sense of gratification or enjoyment; when I had failures it was a deep personal bitterness and sometimes confusion and despair. And there was just something missing in my life—a sense of peace, a sense of higher purpose."

This new awareness of need led Jimmy to do some fresh thinking about God. He had made a profession of faith in Jesus Christ as a youth. He faithfully participated in the life of the Plains Baptist Church. He was a Christian. He knew it. So did most other people.

There had been long talks with his kid sister Ruth when she had helped him campaign out in the Georgia countryside. She had something he didn't have; he knew it. God had worked very powerfully in her life sometime before, restoring her to sound health, mentally and physically, and indeed changing her, and then her husband, veterinarian Robert Stapleton, thoroughly and for the better. She had a deep-rooted relationship with Jesus that produced an unusual freedom and wholeness.

She spoke freely and with remarkable sincerity about having been led to "an experience of God, a loving, caring, personal God, and a Jesus Christ that I had not known in my life as a church member. He was living; he was here and now."

When Jimmy and Ruth prayed together, she spoke as though the Lord were right in the car or the room with them. Ruth seemed to be loving and serving Christ with her whole life. She was the mother of four children, but beyond that she was helping other people, especially troubled people, find peace and inner healing. She seemed to be able to take them right to Jesus, not only for forgiveness, but also for healing and the living of life to its fullest.

If that was possible for her, why not for him? They had grown up together; they had shared many common experiences. She had even been instrumental in his discovering that his childhood friend Rosalynn was the woman he wanted to marry. Ruth was not that much different from him. What did she have that he didn't have?

Other things began to motivate Jimmy Carter to critically re-evaluate his relationship with God. His wife, Rosalynn, told of one instance:

"He had been invited to speak at a church in the county

next to ours about 'witnessing.' So he was sitting in the living room writing out his speech. And he was trying to figure out how many people he had seen in the last ten years for his church. For fourteen years he had always gone with the preacher to see two families before each revival. Ten people a year for fourteen years; that was one hundred and forty people.

"And he had seen thousands, hundreds of thousands for himself as senator and as a candidate for governor."

Carter was not comfortable with the contrast. If he worked so hard for himself—for politics—why did he not work equally hard for the one he knew to be his Lord?

Another example of the sort of influences at work on Carter during this critical period of his life unfolded in his own church in Plains. The thrust came in the title of his pastor's sermon one Sunday. "I do not remember anything our pastor had to say that morning," Carter said, "but I have never forgotten the title of his sermon: 'If You Were Arrested for Being a Christian, Would There Be Enough Evidence to Convict You?' "

Carter found himself "cut to the heart" in much the same manner as those who heard the Apostle Peter preach on the Day of Pentecost. In his book *Why Not the Best?* (p. 132), he said, "I finally decided that if arrested and charged with being a committed follower of God, I could probably talk my way out of it!"

It was an autumn day in Georgia in 1966. Jimmy and his sister Ruth drove through the warm afternoon sunshine into the county of Webster, some miles from Plains. They talked about God and their changing lives as they drove along the quiet road. They wondered about the future, especially Jimmy's.

Driving off the road and leaving the car, they walked into the filtered sunlight of the pine woods, into the quietness and softness. The pine forest was important to Carter. It was part of his environment. He was comfortable there.

Dressed casually, even sloppily, he in khaki trousers and work shirt, she in slacks and shirt, they walked slowly and aimlessly, friends, close friends down through the years, both blond, crinkly-eyed, often smiling. They were hardly aware of the details of their surroundings. The conversation grew more intense. Jimmy was in the process of changing. He needed to share it, to clarify it, to try to understand it.

Ruth told him how she had experienced the release of God's Spirit within her own spirit, the liberation of her being that had come, during a crisis point in her life, some years earlier at a nonsectarian Christian camp meeting. She described her "first step into life worth living" that occurred when she encountered people at that camp who revealed "unconditional love," God's love displayed through His Son, Jesus Christ, by way of the Holy Spirit.

Ruth spoke as though they were two children, sharing their innermost understandings openly, unashamedly, unafraid. Jimmy listened much of the time as they walked. But it was when they had entered into a slight clearing where a large tree had fallen, a place where they stopped to sit awhile, that he asked the question that was burning within him: "What is it that you have that I don't have?"

He was keenly aware of her inner peace, her assurance of her place in the kingdom of God, her sense of the Lord's direction of her life.

"You've got to be willing to accept God's will, no matter what it is," she explained. "It's not that he's going to tell you to do something drastically different; it's just that you've got to have the attitude to be willing to do whatever he wants.

"You've got to look beyond yourself for God's purpose. You've got to be less self-centered in all of your life."

The quietness in the woods gripped them. They seemed alone in the whole world. Ruth went on softly, "Jimmy, you've got to recognize that your mind can't achieve the change you're looking for."

They knelt there in the pine forest, brother and sister physically as well as spiritually, and they prayed together. They asked the Lord Jesus for the grace to conform more exactly to his will for their lives.

Their experience at that moment went beyond politics, beyond being governor, even beyond being president of the United States. It went beyond everything in the world. It was a giant step in the future political leader's move into a new dimension in the Spirit of God. This move was to result, in Carter's words, in "a sense of complete dependence on the Holy Spirit."

The impact of this "deepening experience," as the candidate referred to it during the 1976 campaign, was reflected in many profound ways in the months and years following, but never more publicly than on one day at the height of the primary election season. A questioner, more aptly described as a heckler, rose to challenge Carter. "Just what," he inquired, "is your relationship to Jesus Christ?"

Softly, but clearly, for all present to hear, the candidate replied, "Jesus Christ comes first in my life, even before politics."

"This makes me think," said sister Ruth, when reflecting on that incident, "that Jimmy is still at the same place he was" that day in the piney woods of Georgia.

As Carter's relationship with God deepened, its reality was immediately tested in the opportunity to serve his neighbor. Jesus said, "You shall love the Lord your God with all your heart, and with all your soul, and with all your strength, and with all your mind; and your neighbor as yourself" (Luke 10:27). Carter, and so many others before him, had learned through great distress and anguish that a reversal of the order of those two commands of God will not produce the same results.

"Jimmy had a call one day from the Baptist Brotherhood," his wife said. "It was from somebody in the Southern Baptist Convention, in the office in Atlanta. And they asked him if he would go on a missionary trip.

"He asked them what it would involve. They said: 'Just give a week to the Lord.'

"And he asked: 'Who will pay for it?'

"They said: 'You will.'

"He told them he couldn't do it. He came home and told me about it. And he prayed about it. The next day, I think it was, he called them again and told them he'd do it."

Carter himself spoke of the incident with good-humored enthusiasm. "I was asked by my denominational leaders to go on a pioneer mission effort. On the telephone, I said, 'What am I supposed to do? I don't know anything about mission work.'

"They said, 'You just have to be willing, for a one-week period, to give your life completely to God, with no strings attached.' "

He paused, smiled, and then resumed a serious expression. "At first I said, 'Well, that's easy.' And then I reflected that, although I had been a Christian for thirty years, I had probably never given my life to God with no strings attached for even fifteen minutes."

The pause was even longer. And there was no smile.

"And I went off on this mission later on and got a new perspective for Christianity, what it meant, in a personal way."

The mission effort took Carter with a team to Pennsylvania that year. The Southern Baptist organization is reluctant to disclose precise locations of its missionary work so as not to call excessive attention to itself and also not to embarrass the people with whom it works. We do know, however, that the work Carter participated in was among a group of about one hundred families in which there were no known believers. Traveling in pairs, according to the pattern laid down by Christ with his early disciples, they went door to door, encouraging the people to receive Jesus Christ into their hearts and lives, to be forgiven for their sins, and to enter into new life in Christ.

Although genuine conversions are sometimes difficult to assess on such mission trips, Carter said there were between twenty-five and thirty new professions of faith during the mission.

His wife, Rosalynn, spoke warmly of the change in her husband stemming from his prayer with Ruth and his trip to Pennsylvania. "He called me at home one day and said that he had just put himself completely in God's hands. He was witnessing at the time with a man from Texas who had done this every year, and he was in his seventies. Jimmy said, 'I feel as though if I walked across the street no car would even dare to hit me, because the Lord is with me.' "

The following year found Carter again on a mission in a northern state, this time in Massachusetts, where he worked side by side in a poverty-strained inner city environment with a Cuban minister, Eloy Cruz. They worked primarily among Spanish-speaking people, and Carter's fluency in Spanish, acquired while he was in the navy, served him well.

Carter said he was stirred deeply by the opportunity to serve the people under such conditions—poverty, alienation, hostility—and he was impressed immeasurably by the Christian depth of Cruz, his partner.

"Senor Cruz was a muscular, swarthy, manly person, and one of the best men I have ever known," Carter said later. "He had a remarkable ability to reach the hearts of people in a very natural and unassuming way, and quickly convinced them that we loved them and that God loved them. . . .

"The lives of many people were changed by the words and prayers and laughter and friendship of this good man. . . .

". . . I was saying goodbye to Eloy Cruz, and I asked him how a tough and rugged man like him could be so sensitive, kind, and filled with love. He was embarrassed by my question but finally fumbled out an answer:

". . . 'Our Savior has hands which are very gentle, and he cannot do much with a man who is hard.'

"I thought about this often as governor of Georgia. How

can we combine the competent and efficient management of taxpayers' money with the sensitive and effective service needed to alleviate affliction and to enhance the development and use of the capabilities of our most needy citizens? . . .

". . . Eloy Cruz often said, 'You only need to have two loves: one for God, and one for the person who happens to be standing in front of you at any given moment' " (*Why Not the Best?*, pp. 130-132).

As with so many episodes in the life of a family, there were differences in perception of some minor points in this vital period in Jimmy's life among members of the Carter clan. They all agreed that it was a significant time and that it meant much for the Christian commitment of their most famous member.

But there were interesting differences in how they perceived the relationship of this experience to Carter's continuation in politics. There were moments when Ruth Stapleton, for example, said she thought that her brother was on the verge of continuing indefinitely, perhaps even fulltime, in Christian mission work. She was vividly aware of the kind of impact he was having as he ministered, and she was equally aware of the impact the ministry was having on him.

"Many times when people who had problems would ask him about their problems," she said, "he would refer them to me, and I had long-distance phone calls from people there, saying, 'Are you Jimmy's sister? Well, I'm having this terrible problem in my marriage, and I met your brother up here, and he said you were very good at handling problem situations. He gave me his credit card number and told me to call you.' "

Ruth spoke of an initial, temporary fear that she had, in some way, persuaded Jimmy that, if he were to follow the Lord completely, he would have to give up everything important to him, which, in Jimmy's case, would include politics. Her belief, she said, is that one must be *willing* to give up everything should he be required to do so but that he will not necessarily be asked to do so. But, despite her original concern, she said that after ten years she was not certain that her brother had felt any call to fulltime religious work.

Neither Carter nor his wife recollect that Jimmy ever felt he was being called to abandon politics during that period. It was, in their view, a time of major growth in his Christian experience, of gaining new assurance of God's love. His life had been dramatically altered, so that even politics would not be politics as usual ever again.

4

RESHAPING A STATE

. . . the time for racial discrimination is over.

—Jimmy Carter

It was January, 1971. Rosalynn Carter was seated just to the left of the podium, with little daughter Amy close by her side. The chamber was packed for the inauguration of Georgia's seventy-sixth governor, Jimmy Carter.

In 1966, Carter had lost in his bid for the Democratic gubernatorial nomination to Lester Maddox. It had been one of the most disappointing times in his life, but in less than a month he was back again campaigning for 1970. He later wrote: "I remembered the admonition, 'You show me a good loser and I will show you a loser.' I did not intend to lose again."

So on that inauguration day in January, 1971, he gripped the sides of the lectern and spoke clearly into the microphones:

41

"Our people are the most precious possession. We cannot afford to waste the talents and abilities given by God to one single person. . . . Every adult illiterate, every school drop-out, and every untrained retarded child is an indictment of us all. Our state pays a terrible and continuing human and financial price for these failures. It is time to end this waste. If Switzerland and Israel and other countries can eliminate illiteracy, then so can we.

"At the end of a long campaign, I believe I know the people of this state as well as anyone. Based on this knowledge of Georgians north and south, rural and urban, liberal and conservative, I say to you quite frankly that the time for racial discrimination is over. Our people have already made this major and difficult decision, but we cannot underestimate the challenge of hundreds of minor decisions yet to be made. Our inherent human charity and our religious beliefs will be taxed to the limit. No poor, rural, weak, or black person should ever have to bear the additional burden of being deprived of the opportunity of an education, a job, or simple justice."

And the religious beliefs of the people of Georgia *were* taxed. When they elected Jimmy Carter as their governor, they got more than they bargained for. In the campaign they hadn't taken much notice of Jimmy's faith in God. It didn't seem to count much as an issue with them. After all, professing Christians all over the South talk about the Lord and their faith almost as often and as easily as they talk about their work or their golf game. So the fact that Carter talked freely about being a "born-again Christian" captured little attention in that political contest.

Neither did anyone make much of the fact that the new governor seemed to pray a lot, in fact every day. He used a little room off his office to call upon the Lord about the thousands of decisions facing him as he tried to turn the old, Deep South state around.

But it wasn't long before they were compelled to sit up and take notice, and not only because of Carter's pledge to end discrimination. Other things were happening—the beginnings of the most profound and complete government reorganization ever effected by any state.

The former naval officer had a thesis for what he was undertaking, a thesis he said was developed in prayer, thought and experience, and later expressed in speeches and in writing. One paragraph summarizes it:

"Government at all levels can be competent, economical and efficient. Yet I would hasten to point out that nowhere in the Constitution of the United States, or the Declaration of Independence, or the Bill of Rights, or the Emancipation Proclamation, or the Old Testament, or the New Testament do you find the words 'economy' or 'efficiency.' Not that these two words are unimportant. But you discover other words like honesty, integrity, fairness, liberty, justice, courage, patriotism, compassion, love—and many others which describe the qualities that a human being ought to possess. These are also the same words which describe the qualities that a government of human beings ought to possess."

When he was campaigning, Carter told the voters of Georgia, in effect, that he wanted to be their governor because of the mess that Lester Maddox had left behind. But since he was running on the same ticket with Maddox, who was trying to keep a foot in the door of the state house by running for lieutenant governor, he had to put it a little more politely. What he said was that he thought it "preposterous" that this state—or any state—should be run by the disjointed confusion of 300 semi-independent boards, commissions and agencies. Up to 1971 that was the kind of government to which Georgia had grown accustomed.

So his first major official act as governor, in 1971, was to appoint a team of 117 bright young business and government executives to draft the plans for a new kind of state government. He told the team to ignore all the precedents and traditions of the Georgia government and put together a new government that would be rational and efficient.

The result was the abolition of all 300 of that motley array of boards, commissions, and agencies. Their functions were concentrated in twenty-two new "umbrella" agencies, each with its own unified budget, its own planning and accounting offices and its own carefully screened and tested personnel. When the state legislature rebelled at some of the changes he regarded as most important, Governor Carter went directly to the people. He talked to them by radio and television, and appealed for their support and for their pressure on their own legislative representatives to put his reforms through.

Carter has a stubborn streak, which has been both an asset and a liability at times. In a sober, reflective conversation with a television interviewer, the usually smiling candidate spoke of this and of charges that he was "ruthless" on occasion in dealing with political and legislative problems. He said he considered these accusations wide of the mark.

"I don't think I've ever deliberately hurt one of my opponents to gain an advantage. I try not to," he said. "I don't remember when I have. There may have been something that I said in the heat of competition that made them uncomfortable. I can't deny that. But most people, when they get to know me have finally decided that I'm tougher than is originally apparent."

Regardless, Governor Carter got what he wanted in government reform, but only because some friendly leading legislators stepped in and did some compromising and some apologizing on the governor's behalf.

To fully appreciate all this hard in-fighting, it was necessary to understand that the new governor found compromise very difficult; this springing in part from his commitment to the truth, the whole truth, and not just part of it. He also insists that people must give their best, all the way.

The same thing held true, and still does, for governmental reform. Carter believed that the only effective kind of reform was "reform on a massive scale." He insisted that piecemeal reforms seldom work. And he abhorred what he called "incrementalism," seeing it as a disease that affects legislatures and governments. He explained it this way: "Say an executive tries to make reforms, one tiny phase at a time. Then all those other officials, employees and hangers-on who see their influence being threatened will come out of their rat holes and concentrate on undoing what you are trying to do.

"But if you are bold enough, if you have a proposal that is comprehensive enough to rally the support of the general electorate, then you can overcome the spread of incrementalism, the special-interest-type lobbying pressure."

The governor's stubbornness, his impatience with slow-thinking and slow-acting public officials, nearly got him into trouble another time. It was in 1974, when he was pressuring the legislature to pass a consumer protection law.

Faced with determined opposition that he believed was based on irresponsible grounds, the governor let his usual calm slip for a moment. And he put it on the record that the members of that state legislature were "the worst in the history of the state." This brought action—but the wrong kind. The legislators quit work on the governor's bill for several days, and demanded that he take back his harsh words. Finally, and a little reluctantly, the governor let it be known that he hadn't meant to include all of them in that blanket denunciation. But he never did apologize.

One of his close friends said later that the governor had refused to apologize because he honestly felt his appraisal of the quality of the legislative body, as a whole, was right on the mark.

Georgia state government salaries were kept so low, by law, that some of the best available executives couldn't afford to take jobs in the Carter administration in Atlanta. Others were disappointed because Governor Carter did not hold very firmly to the patronage system. He looked first for the best qualified people for the jobs. For the most important state jobs he almost always reached outside his circle of closest supporters. They seemed to understand this in Georgia. Would they in Washington?

One of his long-time friends and assistants told newsmen about Carter's policies regarding personnel: "Jimmy has a lot of powerful friends around Atlanta who are not on his payroll because he couldn't afford to pay them what they are worth. But they are always ready to help him. That's the kind of loyalty he attracts. And that's how he managed to get good key men to run the government of Georgia in spite of those skinny, inexcusable Georgia state salaries."

Some of the new departments didn't operate as efficiently as expected, but the Carter years in the state house were scandal-free. A special problem among his reforms was the big new Human Resources Department, designed to integrate and deliver all the state's social services. It drew more criticism than all the other reforms together. Even the Carter critics in Georgia admitted, however, that its mistakes were honest mistakes, and that with all its varied failures the Human Resources Department did work better than the old system, which had the social services scattered among a dozen or more different agencies.

The governor got the legislature to approve his government reorganization by a plan that he might well be expected to use in Washington. He presented the legislature with two budgets. One of them showed the costs of government under the existing organization. The other showed what the same services would cost under his reorganization plan.

"We cut administrative costs by fifty percent," Governor Carter said. "We shifted personnel to more productive jobs, and got them away from paper shuffling.

"Though it was highly controversial, it was approved by the legislature. And thirty amendments to the Georgia Constitution were also passed, and later approved by a vote of the people of Georgia.

"Neither the present administration nor the legislature have made any attempt to substantially change Carter's reforms."

Under Governor Carter, Georgia's budget and payroll grew much faster than the national average. The reason, the governor explained, was that the state government had been allowed to stagnate under Governor Maddox. And he quickly added that in spite of the fast-growing budget and payroll there was not a single major tax increase during his four years in office.

Carter also introduced in Georgia what he called the "zero-based" budget system. In his presidential campaign this did not receive much attention, despite the fact he insisted he would take the plan into the Oval Office with him. In brief, the "zero-based" plan requires every government department and agency head to start from scratch and rejustify the continued existence of every government program every year.

Other Carter actions; growing for the most part out of his spiritual perspective on the function of government, were the upgrading of mental hospitals and prisons, the opening of more than one hundred new centers for the mentally retarded, and the initiation of important consumer and environmental programs—areas that had been virtually ignored by previous administrations.

Despite the massive reform and the launching of new programs, the big surprise of the Carter regime was the one signaled in his inauguration speech: "The time for racial discrimination is over." The doors were to be opened to black people in high offices of the state government. The action was unexpected because Carter had not received the support of the blacks in his campaign for governor.

"You won't like my campaign," he had warned one of the Atlanta black leaders, "but you'll be proud of my record as governor."

It was not the kind of campaign that all of his friends

approved. Nor did it fully square with his own attitudes toward compromise in other areas. Carter afterward told some of those friends that he "felt bad" about his actions, and it was known that he had prayed for forgiveness for some of the things that he felt he had had to say and do to get himself elected.

A poll taken by his organization just before the campaign had pictured the mass of Georgia voters as "unyoung, unblack, unpoor, unliberal, anti-establishment and pro-George Wallace." So Carter laid his gubernatorial plans accordingly.

His opponent was former Governor Carl Sanders, a popular figure, but suspect in "red neck" quarters of having "liberal ideas." So, according to Georgians who watched it all, Carter portrayed himself as a sort of intellectual "red neck" and his opponent as the pawn of Atlanta money and an admirer of Hubert Humphrey liberalism. A photo of Mr. Sanders being doused with champagne by two black Atlanta basketball players also appeared mysteriously all over the state. Carter insisted that he knew nothing about it, and he still holds to that. But rumor had it that the episode could be explained by his young campaign manager, Hamilton Jordan, just out of college and still filled with enthusiasm for the college type of prank.

In the course of the campaign, Carter uttered some more or less faint words of praise for the man who shared the Democratic ticket with him, segregationist Maddox. He said later, however, that they were enemies then, and always have been. He also told one large campaign audience in Atlanta that he would invite another noted segregationist, Governor George Wallace of Alabama, to speak for him in the state. Further, only five days before the election, he ostensibly gave his blessing to private schools, set up to avoid integration of education, by visiting one of them, accompanied by reporters and cameramen.

It was unquestionably a campaign of expedience. And it worked. Carter confessed it all later—to friends and to the Lord. "I often had to compromise," he said. "But I didn't compromise in a back room. My purpose was to spread out my position openly. You know, I have temptations, to which I sometimes yield. But I don't think Georgia suffered under my administration because of that attitude. . . ."

Carter got the votes of most of the "hard hats" and the "wool hats" but only about five percent of the black vote in that 1970 election. He won by a landslide, although, to many of the groups that supported him, his record of action looked more like an earthquake. The new governor had portraits of Martin Luther King, Jr. and other black leaders hung in the capitol, while the Ku Klux Klan picketed angrily outside. He fell into open war with Maddox. Furthermore, he dismissed one of his leading segregationist supporters, Roy Harris, from the State Board of Regents. He also began filling some good jobs in state government with black people.

The governor's abrupt switch, or at least what they thought was his abrupt switch, stunned both his supporters and those who had opposed him. But as months passed, and it became apparent that, in reality, the governor was a moderate, not wholly committed to either side, his former supporters cooled their anger, and his former opponents, especially the blacks, warmed toward him.

Governor Carter then, as now, refused to accept a label. Gradually, he acquired the image of "Mr. Clean," in an era of politics and patronage. He showed a preference for public confrontation as against private horse-trading.

His executive assistant in the governor's office, Mr. Jordan, told of a time when one of the legislators came to the governor seeking a promotion for his father-in-law. "We needed his vote, so we asked the governor to do it. He refused, and here we were, idealistic young kids, urging him to be more political. He told us he didn't spend four years of his life running for governor just to promote some guy's father-in-law. And that was that."

5

THE DECISION

*. . . we were considering
whether this was what he wanted
to do, what he should do.*

—Rosalynn Carter

Jimmy Carter was wearing blue jeans and a tee shirt, and
he was barefoot. It was not unusual attire for this governor
of Georgia, particularly on a warm August night, even in the
governor's mansion in Atlanta. He often relaxed that way.
But this night, in 1972, was not an ordinary night.

He was welcoming five old friends, people already close to
him and destined to be much closer. They had struggled
valiantly and smartly to clear the way to the governorship
for Carter through the political thickets of the state of Georgia. There was Hamilton Jordan, campaign manager and
number one gubernatorial aide, Jody Powell, press secretary and intimate friend; Gerald Rafshoon, advertising man
and media adviser; Landon Butler, Atlanta businessman
and conservationist; and Dr. Peter Bourne, head of a state
drug abuse program.

They were comfortable with the governor, and he with them. Lounging in easy chairs scattered casually around the room, they got to the point of their visit without preliminaries.

"We are convinced you should run for president," they said.

They told friends later that they had expected the governor to shake his head and deliver a firm "No." But he didn't. In fact, they said, he was far ahead of them. Carter had been thinking about the same idea and already had talked it over and prayed about it with an even more intimate group and had reached about the same conclusion as the five visitors to the executive mansion.

The only serious difficulty was one that they later chuckled about. It was the problem of merely using the word "president." It felt awkward to them and they felt presumptuous when they said it, so they tried to find ways to talk without using the word. Carter himself said, "We were at first embarrassed about the use of the word 'president.' There was something that was so exalted in my mind about the office of president that it was hard for me to say that in the same sentence with my own name."

But they conquered their reticence and began to talk, earnestly and candidly, about the possibility. There would be difficulties for a man from the South, but that could be turned around by emphasizing that it's a "New South." There would be grumbling about lack of Washington experience, but that could be an asset in the wake of the Watergate scandals and the public's distrust of the Washington establishment.

Carter later told about "the feeling that the government, as we presently knew it, was not measuring up to the honesty, integrity, the idealism, the compassion, the love, and expectations of the American people."

He said that feeling was the biggest factor in their thoughts and in the ultimate decision. "We had been through Vietnam, Cambodia; we were going through various stages of Watergate, and the people were disillusioned about the government—and legitimately so, because the government just wasn't as good as our people were."

And that's the way it went, into the night. The longer they talked, the less awesome seemed the proposition. For one thing, Carter's faith, although not shared on the same level by all those present, was nonetheless infectious.

As young Jordan and the others left the mansion in the late hours, they knew they were on the brink of decision. Two or three steps lay just ahead of them. One was to be taken by Jordan—"Put it on paper," Carter told him as he departed. Other steps were to be taken by Jimmy, his wife, and his children—"We'll have to pray and talk about it," he said.

Few knew it, but there were others Carter was talking to about this plan and about other important things in his life.

One relative told of "Jimmy's small group . . . the ones Jimmy can say anything to—can let down with. They provide him with Christian undergirding and support."

The governor was accustomed to occasional "Sunday night suppers" in which he would share with those with whom he was most at ease. They were men who shared the spiritual dimension of his life. They were men who were, for the most part, deeply committed to Jesus Christ; men who not only talked together, but also prayed together.

They were, in fact, part of the answer to a question that was often heard among Christians during the presidential primary campaign: "Why doesn't Jimmy Carter have more committed Christians around him? The questioners saw only staff members and other aides who showed little, if any, spiritual commitment. But, behind these scenes, especially at times of decision, the picture was more prayerful. This did not always please the "up-front" people, but Carter persisted.

Among those confidants with whom he shared most intimately his life in Christ and his dependence on the will of God, were:

—Philip Alston, a banker who is described as "the most benevolent man in Atlanta," and thoroughly committed to Jesus Christ.

—David Gambrell, who was treasurer of Carter's early campaigns and who was named to fulfill the unexpired term in the United States Senate upon the death of the late Richard B. Russell. He was described by one former campaign worker as a man who "would just pray-in the money in those days when we didn't have any." Through what was described as a misunderstanding, there was a rift between him and Carter during Gambrell's campaign for his own senate term.

—Bill Milliken, a Christian youth worker whose relationship with Carter began unexpectedly when the governor helped get money for Milliken's highly successful program for combating drug abuse.

—Bill Gunter, a lawyer from Gainesville, Georgia.

—Robert Lipshutz, an Atlanta lawyer and Jewish leader, who despite differences in faith, maintained a deep spiritual affinity with Carter and his Christian friends. He went on to become treasurer of the presidential campaign and was described by one close to the Carter family as "a man with a great spiritual quality."

In the Carter family, the conviction that the governor should run for the Democratic nomination did not come overnight. "I can't remember a specific scene when I decided to run for president," Carter said. "It was a slow realization during 1972 when I met the other candidates for president and when I had also met my first president, who was Richard Nixon."

Meanwhile, Mrs. Carter and their three sons started talking about the idea during the 1972 presidential campaign when the candidates began their march through Georgia. They usually came to the governor's mansion for dinner and often to spend the night. They were examined at close range and were seen for just what they were: people, quite ordinary people. Among them were Nixon, Spiro Agnew, George McGovern, Henry Jackson, Hubert Humphrey, Edmund Muskie, George Wallace, Ronald Reagan, Nelson Rockefeller, and others.

Getting a close look at these leading public figures convinced the Carter family that the head of their household was at least as qualified as these men for the presidency of the United States. Carter himself said he came to the "slow realization . . . that I was equal to them—not better than anybody else—but equal to them." The other members of the family felt even more strongly. They were certain he was more qualified than anybody they had seen.

Even so, no one in the family remembered any specific time that they sat down together and agreed that Carter should run. It was a decision that crept up on them, one that they came to recognize finally as the right one.

Mrs. Carter reconstructed the period like this:

"It was an idea that we first started talking about in 1971, I think it was, when the candidates for the presidency started coming through Georgia. My boys were already men then, and we—my boys and I—decided that Jimmy knew a lot more about a lot of things than did these men who were running for president. And about then different people began mentioning to Jimmy that he should run for president.

"There wasn't any one day that he called the family together and said, 'I'm going to run for president.' I remember only that we talked about it and prayed about it. Then, along toward the end of 1972—we had been thinking about it for a long time by then—we were considering whether this was what he wanted to do, what he should do. And that's when we really started praying about it. It was some time between Thanksgiving and Christmas. That is when he definitely decided. It was a gradual thing."

In 1972, the governor's family spent several days of the Thanksgiving season on the Georgia coast. It was a relaxed, quiet time.

Into that scene strode the confident aide, Hamilton Jordan, then twenty-eight years old, armed with the memo he had been instructed to prepare on why the governor should run for the presidential nomination in 1976. The seventy-page document he had prepared, which was examined in minute detail during that holiday at the seashore, turned out to be prophetic in many respects.

One significant point in the memo fit Carter to perfection. It was that voters were looking first for integrity—quality—not a specific stand on issues. Jordan's thesis was that voters were looking beyond issues. They were looking for someone to believe in, and that's where Carter stood out most strongly.

Furthermore, he argued, the voters wanted competence, and Governor Carter had a strong record in reorganizing and running the government of Georgia and, before that, the building of his own successful business.

Then, the "not-from-Washington" theme was popular and spreading in many parts of the country. That theme, he wrote, lent itself to some first-rate sloganeering, backed up by the other themes of "honesty," "competence," "no-ties-to-the-establishment," and the like.

By Christmas, the final decision was made. Jimmy would run. The Christmas holidays for the Carters at the governor's mansion had an extra tingle that year. The excitement was low-key, but it was there, along with a sense of awe and intrigue.

The family, however, punctured every threat of inflation in the Carter ego. Jimmy's mother, "Miz Lillian," for example, when soberly confronted by her son and told, "Mother, I'm going to run for president," replied: "President of what?"

But they were all with him in this as they always have been through times of personal difficulty. The individual Carter family members do not maintain especially close contact—they are not eager letter writers or regular telephone callers—but they stand together when there is a need.

In the end, the decision to run was for Jimmy and Rosalynn to make. By all accounts, they came to the final moment of choice quietly and prayerfully.

When he was asked which particular person's opinion weighed most heavily in that final moment, Carter said gently and in great seriousness: "Well, I guess that was my wife. She's been a partner with me in everything I've ever done. She's the only woman that I've ever loved, and I think she agreed with my decision from the very beginning."

As for the substance of that final decision, the soft-spoken Georgian described it this way: "I have never felt that the Lord required me to run for president, or that I'm ordained to be president. I don't have that feeling at all. But I pray about all the decisions in my life that have any significance, and I have the feeling, without any doubt at all, that what I'm doing is compatible with God's will, whether I should win or lose. There's no doubt in my mind that my campaign for the presidency is what God wants me to do."

The governor's tiny, brunette wife is soft and womanly in appearance. But this hides the toughness and strength she showed in the presidential primary race, both as a campaigner and a key decision-maker. She was asked why she believed, in 1972, that it was God's will for her husband to run for the nomination. Her reply:

"Well, his term as governor was up [at the end of 1974, and he could not succeed himself], our business was running well at home, and he was deeply concerned about the country. He was praying about whether he should run for president, and it came to him that God wants us to use our talents.

"But he never prayed that he would be president. He prayed that he would do what was right, and that God would guide him in the whole experience."

6

OFF AND RUNNING

*Our strategy was simple: make a
total effort all over the nation.*

—Jimmy Carter

Carter said it simply: "There's no doubt in my mind that
my campaign for the presidency is what God wants me to
do." But there were four years of prayer and preparation
behind him when he said it.

His wife, Rosalynn, filled in a few of the details: "He
studied everything," she says. "He read books about all the
presidents. He even read a book about those who ran for
president and lost. He studied the issues of government. He
put together information on every possible issue he could
think of. I remember we bought a jigsaw puzzle that was a
map of the United States—to learn the locations of the
states."

But he realized that knowing the country was not enough;
the country had to know him. Some of the national Democratic leaders were vaguely aware that he was one of those

The Miracle of Jimmy Carter

"New South" governors that *The New York Times Sunday Magazine* was always writing about, and raving about. But right up until the day of his formal announcement as a candidate, at the end of 1974, most of the voters had never heard of him.

"Our strategy," he wrote in his book, *Why Not The Best?* (p. 141), "was simple: make a total effort all over the nation." As an aide put it: "The idea was to run everywhere, go everywhere and meet everybody." They counted on the Carter charm and personality to do the rest.

To underline that Washington had no strings on him, it was decided that the Carter campaign headquarters would be in Atlanta. It cost the Carter people a lot of long-distance phone bills, but it worked.

Then came a coincidence that may or may not have been a coincidence—an unexpected, and probably unintended boost from the Democratic National Committee.

Carter was chosen by the National Committee chairman, Robert S. Strauss, for what usually is a largely honorary job, the chairmanship of the national party's Committee to Elect Democrats to Congress in 1974. Strauss said later that he felt, at the time, that Carter, of all people, would have no reason to use the job to promote himself among the party leaders in the various states. He knows, now, that he was wrong, but he says he has no regrets about the appointment.

"Carter took off as if he were being chased," says press secretary Jody Powell, "and before he stopped he had gone to thirty states, pitched in to help sixty-two candidates, and contacted party leaders in one way or another in the other twenty states."

He came home, after the election, with a stack of political IOU's in his briefcase and with oceans of goodwill left behind him. He paid for most of that travel himself.

Hamilton Jordan, Carter's thirty-one-year-old campaign manager this year, was detached from his job as the governor's administrative assistant to go to Washington and work with Carter on his National Committee assignment in '74. "It gave Jimmy an excuse to go into places like Iowa and

New Hampshire, which were important to his early momentum this year," he said. "And besides," he added, "we learned a lot about the rest of the country, and Jimmy did a good job."

Strauss, a jovial, but tough-talking Texan, still laughingly speaks of the Carter appointment as "letting the Trojan Peanut into the National Committee encampment." But wife, Rosalynn, insists somewhat indignantly that Carter didn't abuse the appointment. "Jimmy was still governor," she points out, "and he only worked on this election job on weekends. He would leave on Friday night and come back on Sunday night. . . . He got to know a lot of people."

Nobody in Washington, up to the election of 1974, had any idea of what was being planned in Atlanta. Carter's little "Gideon's Army" of political novices, most of them in their twenties or early thirties, was frantically preparing for the attack. The Bible tells us Gideon won his war with 300 men. Carter launched his with the help of only ten men and two women. There were more later, but never more than two-hundred, scattered over the whole country.

Carter is a natural-born "motivator." His sister Ruth puts it this way: "I got so mad. I get around him, and I'm a hundred times more committed to him than I was. Then I come home (to North Carolina) and get to doing my things, and then I go back and it happens all over again. He pulls out of you everything you've got, to the last breath. He doesn't mean to. I mean—he's that kind of person."

Most of the nucleus of Carter's campaign staff are Georgians; many of them have been with him since early in his political career. Their backgrounds, in most cases, do not suggest that they might be successful operatives in a campaign to take over the White House. But the voters will decide that in November. Here are the troops that were in at the start with "Gideon" Carter:

Hamilton Jordan

Jordan, only thirty-one in the election year, was still in college when he first joined the Carter group, in 1966. He remembers that he had a job that summer spraying places that were breeding mosquitoes, and he just happened into a campaign meeting while Carter was in the midst of his losing campaign for governor. The then State Senator Carter was impressed by the young man and recruited him to work with young people in the campaign.

Jordan says now, "It was good that Jimmy lost that race. He was the kind of guy who never failed before, and it was rough on him, but it probably did him good." Young Jordan left for a two-year stint in Vietnam with the International Volunteer Service after the campaign. He got back to Georgia just in time to help in the successful 1970 race for the governorship, and he was appointed the governor's executive secretary. A native of Albany, Georgia, Jordan has been the Carter campaign manager and chief of staff since the start of the presidential race. He is an easy-going, courtly southerner, and his job was to see that everything ran smoothly. He left strategy and issues to the governor and other aides.

Jody Powell

The thirty-two-year-old Carter press secretary, a native of Vienna, Georgia, was believed by others on the staff to have a closer relationship with Carter than anyone other than the governor's wife. He was a political science graduate student at Emory University in Atlanta in 1969 when he met Carter. At the time, he was writing a paper on the development of a Wallace third party, and he was stressing the reasons why such a party should not be the inheritor of the South. Later that same year, he wrote a letter to Carter about his paper and about some of the problems he foresaw in the gubernatorial campaign. He offered his help.

Carter wrote a long letter in reply and invited him and a half-dozen others to his home in Plains to discuss the campaign and possible pitfalls. Then only twenty-six, Jody signed on. He said later that he did it "because that part of the state—southern Georgia—has been known as an area that produces a different sort of politician; men noted mainly for bombastic rhetoric, exploitation of the race issue and all that. And this was a chance to show the world and the rest of the state that everybody wasn't like that."

For five months, Carter and Powell traveled everywhere together, mainly by car. As Powell described it, "We would drive into a courthouse square, and while Mr. Carter got out and shook hands, I would take down names to be phoned back to Atlanta for a political follow-up."

Although different in style and widely separate in age, the governor and his press secretary, partly as a result of long conversations on their campaign trips, became close friends.

Carter was outwardly shy and withdrawn, more serious and orderly, more inner directed and self-contained. Powell was fun-loving, slightly irreverent, more casually efficient than orderly, but open, friendly and possessed of a good sense of humor.

One common tie was that they had both attended service academies. Carter was an Annapolis graduate; Powell was an undergraduate at the Air Force Academy until he was expelled in his senior year for a violation of the honor code in an examination. Powell admitted this charge, telling Carter about it before he was hired. The candidate was reported to have told him to forget it.

During the Carter administration in Atlanta, Powell served as press secretary and also ran the legal office, heading up the drafting of legislation, and lobbying for its passage. He also worked on the governor's appointments. He was a trouble-shooter on issues and was the only man authorized to speak for Carter.

He did not have journalistic experience, and when one of the top staff members was asked why the governor had picked him to do the press job, he scratched his head and replied: "He just seemed the most appropriate man."

Rosalynn Carter

The candidate's wife was forty-eight years old during the campaign and did not flinch when acknowledging it. But to thousands who saw her indefatigable campaigning the thought must have occurred that "the lady is overstating her age."

Mrs. Carter is not only the candidate's wife of thirty years, but also his "best friend." Both the campaign manager and the press secretary agreed that Rosalynn, as friend and adviser, plays a supremely important role in her husband's life. She and three of her four children spent months traveling the country on their own, giving the impression that "the Carters are everywhere." She saw her husband only rarely, but they talked daily and sometimes oftener by phone. They talked over nuts-and-bolts politics like two experienced politicians.

"She doesn't get involved in the planning of strategy," Powell said, "but she is invaluable as a campaigner because she has terrific political instinct. Also, she's a good judge of character and good at picking people for sensitive jobs. Jimmy leans heavily on her judgment."

Jordan called her "a very savvy woman."

"I don't admit this to the governor," he said, "but whenever I have trouble with him on a decision, and he's being stubborn and I think he's wrong, I go to work on Rosalynn."

Charles Kirbo

The elder statesman of the Carter camp is Charles Kirbo, fifty-nine, a country lawyer from Banbridge, Georgia, who won the admiration of Carter in 1962, when he saved Jimmy's state senate candidacy from defeat by winning a ballot-stuffing case for him. He was a Carter regular from then on and became a close friend.

Kirbo's function in the campaign was as sort of an intermediary between the governor and his staff. He was described as "the closest thing the governor has to a peer, who can talk to him as an equal." Kirbo described himself as "the old man of the Carter movement."

He was Democratic state chairman in Georgia for a short time during the Carter administration, and he served the governor as a talent scout. Asked what role he would play if Carter was elected, Kirbo shrugged and said he'd help if he was wanted, but added, "I'm just a bush-leaguer."

"Jimmy has a lot of powerful help around Atlanta that's

not on his payroll," Kirbo confided. "They're substantial-type people we couldn't afford if we had to pay them. And you won't see their names on any doors. But he's always had them."

Among this high-priced but voluntary help, according to Kirbo, were Philip Alston, the Atlanta banker and confidant; Bert Lance, a banker who headed the highway department when Carter was governor; Jack Watson, a Kirbo partner; and Brooks Pennington, a feed-grain businessman in Madison, Georgia.

Andrew Young

Andrew Young is the United States representative from Atlanta. One of the most influential blacks in the South, Young, at forty-four, was adviser to Governor Carter not only on black affairs, but also on politics generally.

Young, a former executive director of the Southern Christian Leadership Conference under the late Martin Luther King, Jr., is one of the most effective orators in Congress. He was the first major black leader to come to Carter's support; he helped quiet the storm stirred up by the "ethnic purity" remark by forcefully reminding the black people of Carter's friendliness toward them when he held power in the state of Georgia. He traveled extensively with the candidate and, in the opinion of staff members, was headed for higher things in any Carter administration.

Robert Lipshutz

This was the money man, the campaign treasurer. Fifty-four-year-old Lipshutz is an Atlanta lawyer, a leader in the city's Jewish community, and a close friend of the candidate. When Carter was governor, he served on the State Human Resources Board. He was a major political adviser during the campaign along with his fund-raising and fund-accounting duties.

He was a Carter man since before the 1966 defeat in the bid for the governorship and helped map the radical reform of the Georgia state government, which was Carter's chief accomplishment as governor.

Lipshutz was not new at the money-raising business. He

helped raise money to finance Carter's travels during his 1974 tenure on the Democratic National Committee's congressional campaign group.

Jerry Rafshoon

He was the governor's "ad man and media adviser" and television expert. Rafshoon, who operated a successful Atlanta advertising agency, was the man who got Carter off to an early start in television commercials, by getting into filming nearly a year ahead of any of the governor's rivals.

He was forty-two years old and had been close to Carter since the governor ran his losing campaign in 1966. He is a graduate of the University of Texas and was with the Lyndon B. Johnson television station in Austin, Texas.

Peter Bourne

Dr. Bourne was Carter's man in Washington. At thirty-six years of age, he headed the organizing effort for Carter in the District of Columbia area and was frequently host to the governor when he visited the capital.

Dr. Bourne headed a drug abuse program for Governor Carter and was one of the early backers of his plan to run for president. Born in England, he was a graduate of Emory University Medical School in Atlanta and claimed to be a naturalized Georgian. He was a practicing psychiatrist in Washington during the campaign.

Dr. Bourne met Carter in 1969 while working with Mrs. Carter on a mental health program.

Betty Rainwater

Twenty-nine-year-old Betty was the governor's deputy press secretary, working with Powell and traveling with the governor when Powell had a call to duty in Atlanta or elsewhere.

Miss Rainwater was teaching music and ballet in a high school before she joined the campaign in 1975. It was a return engagement—she had also worked in the governor's successful 1970 campaign. Like Powell, she was not a journalist and had no newspaper or other media experience. But, also like Powell, she "just seemed the most appropriate" person for the job when the choice was made.

Off and Running

Greg Schneiders

At twenty-eight, Schneiders was a successful businessman. Before working as Carter's personal traveling aide, he was a Georgetown University dropout, the operator of Whitby's Restaurant on Capitol Hill in Washington, and later the owner of the Georgetown Beef Company. He sold both of those successful businesses to become a professional food service consultant in the District of Columbia.

A quiet, firm and resourceful aide-de-camp, Schneiders was the first man to see the candidate in the morning and the last to see him at night, except for the ever-present Secret Service detail. He was responsible for keeping him on schedule and for getting him to appointments on time. He said the only time the governor lost his cool was when circumstances beyond his control put him appreciably off schedule.

Rick Hucheson

During the primary campaign period, at the age of twenty-four, he was Carter's chief delegate-hunter. He was assistant director of political research at the Democratic National Committee when Carter and Jordan were running the congressional campaign committee in 1974.

A District of Columbia native and a graduate of Swarthmore, Hucheson was studying for a Ph.D. at the University of California when he was offered—and took—the National Committee job. Jordan recruited him and assigned him the task of finding out how delegates were selected in the various states, and how Carter could get his name on every ballot available.

Frank Moore

Another of the team of Georgians, forty-year-old Frank Moore, was Carter's campaign chairman for the entire South during the primaries.

He had worked with the governor since his successful bid for the governorship in 1970 and succeeded Jordan as executive secretary in the Carter administration. He first met Carter in 1966 while working for the Georgia Mountain Planning and Development Commission.

Meanwhile, there was an amusing facet to the mighty rush of the Carter express, although it didn't begin to manifest itself until the primary election season. Its backdrop was the fact that just about everybody in Washington agreed on at least one thing: Nobody who lived outside of Washington could really be well informed.

This was a source of comfort to a somewhat dazed Washington establishment when "that little man from Georgia" began to climb in the political polls. "Any day now he'll put his foot in his mouth, and then he'll wish he had stayed down on the peanut farm." That was the reassurance passed across the Georgetown dinner tables and whispered knowingly at cocktail parties. "What can he know of the inner workings of the federal government; about tax policy, budget problems, national security, defense? Even more unlikely, does he know anything at all about foreign affairs?"

Those were the questions, brushed off with a shrug in January, but asked with more concern in February, and with increasing urgency as Carter won in New Hampshire, Florida, North Carolina, and then in Illinois, Wisconsin, Pennsylvania, Texas, Indiana, Georgia, Alabama and finally right in Washington itself, where Carter walked away with the District of Columbia primary election.

There was suspicion that somebody on the "inside" had defected and was "leaking" knowledge that should be known only to the capital elite. Carter was confounding hostile press questioners with answers that showed a current and comprehensive grasp of the whole galaxy of public affairs, foreign and domestic.

Finally, the worst fears of the self-assured Washingtonians were confirmed. In the closing hours of the crucial Carter sweep in Pennsylvania it was disclosed that a host of the country's most knowledgeable experts in many fields had quietly—and voluntarily—begun to support Carter. Together they comprised a brain trust of awesome weight. They had come, of their own volition, to advise him in the campaign, and in the White House.

But this made the Carter picture more confusing than ever, especially to the pundits of journalism who were trying to put a label on him. Even by monitoring his advisers, it was still impossible to tell where Carter stood. That was because he had acquired advisers on *both* sides of almost every major question. And he thus avoided the bad political mistake made by President Ford near the start of the campaign, when he fired his knowledgeable secretary of defense because the secretary disagreed with, and argued in cabinet meetings with, his secretary of state.

The Washington elite learned some other surprising things, too, after the dust had settled in Pennsylvania. They learned that Carter, as early as 1973, while he was still governor of Georgia, had been spotted by David Rockefeller, president of the Chase Manhattan Bank, as a rising figure. He was recruited that year by Rockefeller to represent the southern half of the United States on the prestigious Trilateral Commission. This was an exclusive forum of world thought and discussion that included in its membership political leaders, top foreign policy intellectuals, and leading businessmen of North America, Western Europe and Japan.

It came to light also that for the last year or more Carter, personally, and his top staff assistants had been coached at the Brookings Institution in Washington by a team of experts in all phases of government. Brookings, of course, had not turned itself over to the Carter camp; it opened the doors of its vast storehouse of knowledge to all legitimate presidential aspirants. But Carter and his group were using it more than anyone else. There were almost daily calls from the Carter headquarters in Atlanta to the Brookings.

So confident of final success were the Carter advisers and assistants that there was an increasing scramble for positions close to the nominee, with an eye on eventual administration jobs.

Zbigniew Brzezinski, Columbia University's Russian Affairs expert, who is also director of the Trilateral Commission, was one of the few almost certainly scheduled for high-level administration jobs.

Half-jokingly, a Carter adviser said there were three different status badges among the growing legion of Carter advisers and helpers: "The Chosen, the Anointed, and the Converted."

"The Chosen" were those who had been at the governor's side since the presidential drive started in 1972. "The Anointed" included, roughly, the advisers who rallied to his banner in 1975, before it became obvious that he would be a winner. "The Converted" came aboard after the New Hampshire primary.

An early indication that Carter intended to keep his mind open was the news that his earliest advisers on defense affairs were Paul Warnke, a high Pentagon official in the Johnson Administration, and Paul Nitze, who was a deputy secretary of defense under Secretary Robert S. McNamara. Nitze was a hawk on nuclear weapons policy; Warnke's views came close to those of Morris Udall, the liberal candidate.

Others in the unofficial Carter "brain trust" included:

W. Averell Harriman, an elder statesman of American diplomacy and former ambassador to the Soviet Union. He joined the Carter advisers in early May.

Cyrus Vance was a deputy secretary of defense under McNamara and a member of the New York law firm of Simpson, Thacher and Bartlett.

Theodore Sorensen, a top speechwriter for John F. Kennedy, the man who drafted the early Kennedy speeches of commitment to the war in Vietnam.

Richard Holbrooke, managing editor of *Foreign Policy* magazine, and Anthony Lake, executive director of International Volunteer Service. Both held important State Department and White House positions until they became opposed to prolonging the Vietnam War under the Nixon-Kissinger policies of the early 1970s.

Richard Gardner, a colleague of Brzezinski at Columbia

University, devoted a generous amount of time coaching Carter early in his drive toward the presidency, at a time when not many were willing to acknowledge the former governor had a chance.

Stuart Eizenstadt, an Atlanta attorney and long-time friend and adviser of Carter.

Henry Owen, director of foreign policy studies at Brookings Institution and former head of the State Department's Policy Planning Staff. In his Brookings position, Owen was obliged to avoid taking sides in the political arena. He gave help equally to all of the candidates who asked for it. Eventually, after frequent contacts with the candidate, he joined the Carter foreign policy task force. He set up a series of briefings at the Brookings Institution for Carter and his policy helpers. Two of the Brookings people who conducted the briefings also later joined the task force: Barry Blechman, a former member of the staff of the Center for Naval Analysis, and C. Fred Bergsten, formerly an official of the National Security Council under Kissinger, and an expert on international economic affairs. Carter was briefed extensively, in addition, by another Brookings man, Ed Fried, a noted expert on international energy questions.

Owen emphasized that, although he was voluntarily a Carter brain-truster, his advice was still available to the Republicans. "If Ronald Reagan had walked through our door and asked our advice, we would have provided it," he said. "But he didn't."

Lawrence Robert Klein, fifty-five, president-elect of the American Economic Association and Benjamin Franklin Professor at the Wharton School of the University of Pennsylvania, had agreed to advise Carter on economics. His specialty was making economic forecasts on precise mathematical equations.

Klein told newsmen that he had been wary of taking the job with Carter because other candidates he tried to advise in 1968 and 1972 hadn't even read the position papers he gave them. But he noted: "When I talked with Carter last

November he showed that he had read the materials I'd sent him. He listened to what I had to say, and asked good questions."

In an important way, the gathering together of a large number of persons, known to have divergent views, was a major political plus for Carter. It proved to official Washington, to the doubters, to many who were wavering on the verge of coming to his support, that this outsider from Georgia was willing to listen to advice, that he had the ability to attract talented people, and that persons of known high intelligence and expertise were willing to acknowledge Carter as their "leader" and "boss."

The candidate after church in Plains, Georgia.

Jimmy as a fifteen-year-old.

Jimmy returns to "the red soil of Georgia" where he relaxes on patio with mother, Lillian; wife, Rosalynn; and youngest child, Amy.

Charles Rafshoon Photo

Carter the farmer.

Charles Rafshoon Photo

Carter the hunter.

An embrace from the Rev. Martin Luther King Sr.

The serious-minded candidate.

Roger F. Hicks II Photo

Rosalynn the campaigner.

All smiles after 1970 gubernatorial victory.

A hand for the Star-Spangled Banner.

7

REVIVING THE NATION

The people . . . in this country deserve to have a government as good, honest and moral as they are.

—Jimmy Carter

For more than eighteen months before he won the presidential nomination, Carter traveled the fifty states, preaching the need for a moral revival in high places. The basic issue of 1976, in the view of the Democratic nominee, was the decay of morality and the decline of honesty in government. "The people of the country feel they've been betrayed," he said. "They don't understand why something is going on in our nation's government that's a matter of embarrassment and shame. The competence of government is not an accepted characteristic any more. No matter what a person hopes to do ultimately in life, no matter what his top hope or aspiration might be, he feels, generally, that Washington is an obstacle to the realization of that hope, rather than an asset to be tapped in the future, in the consummation of that hope."

"Yet," he added, "the people in this country are intensely patriotic; they love their government so much it hurts. They deserve to have a government as good, honest and moral as they are."

And that, in essence, was why this modest "born-again" Christian from southern Georgia wanted to be sent to the White House. He believed that all over America people understood what he was saying. He hoped that millions of them would vote for him.

But, at the same time, he felt puzzlement and some frustration because of a widely prevalent notion that he was not saying plainly what he thought, what he planned to do when—and he always said "when" not "if"—he was elected. But, in truth, there is a massive, almost encyclopedic record of Carter's ideas, views, proposals and promises (although he does not make many promises), all as spoken by him. Most of it was spoken on the campaign trail, some in speeches, some in press conferences, and it provides a good outline of his strategy for reviving the nation. Following are excerpts from that strategy:

Planning in Government

One important thing that's always been left out [of government reforms] is long-range planning.

When I was elected governor of Georgia we wrote down exactly what we wanted to accomplish in mental health, physical health, education, alcoholism, drug control, prison reform, tax reform, transportation, etc., at the end of one year, two years, five years, twenty years.

We estimated cost figures on it for the first five years.

This is the kind of approach I would bring to the White House. I'd say, "This is what our nation hopes to achieve at the end of these periods of time."

The Welfare Mess

We've got about twelve million people on welfare—permanently.

We've got two million welfare workers; that's one worker for every six recipients. Good people, but they don't spend their time alleviating suffering, or dealing with the aged, or helping people get a job who are out of work.

They spend their time in offices, bogged down in red tape, shuffling papers, trying to administer about one hundred different welfare programs.

All my advisers agree, you need to simplify the whole system.

Remove from welfare those people who can work full time. That's about 1.3 million people. Put them under the responsibility of the Labor Department, the Education Department. Treat them as temporarily unemployed people.

The other ninety percent can't work full time; they ought to stay under the welfare system.

There ought to be one nationwide welfare payment to meet the necessities of life—varying in amount only to accommodate the cost of living. This varies from one community to another.

There ought to be a "work incentive" aspect built in, which is now absent.

If a mother has two little children and her husband is dead and she can leave these youngsters with a grandmother for fifteen hours a week, she ought to be encouraged to get a part-time job, and not have her welfare payments confiscated.

We ought to remove the elements of the welfare law that encourage or force a father to leave home.

And cut down the number of programs [from one hundred or more] to no more than one or two.

That would eliminate the food stamp program.

Just one basic payment would mean a great deal.

Education

I would give all revenue-sharing funds to local governments [cutting out the state governments as the middlemen]. [I would] change the revenue-sharing law to remove the prohibitions against using the money for things like day care centers, education, preventive health care.

I think we are going to see, inevitably, a rapid growth in the percentage of payments to education coming from the federal government, because I think the local governments are overburdened with regressive taxes—sales taxes, property taxes and the like.

The natural growth in income in the future is inevitably in the federal tax structure.

I would favor heavy orientation of the federal portion of the education funds toward children who are deprived in some way.

Urban Problems

I would not favor the federal government ever injecting itself between a state and a local government.

In the New York City problem, which is illustrative, I did not favor guaranteeing New York City's bonds.

I would have favored keeping New York City and the state bound together, with a mutual responsibility, and requiring only two things: (1) that the budget be balanced sometime in the future, as assessed and monitored, and (2) that the bonds that have already been sold or are to be sold be sound.

Under those circumstances I would have guaranteed New York State's bonds from the federal government, under which circumstances they would not have been taxed any further.

I don't know how long it would take [to balance New York City's budget], but I'll say this: As soon as I'm president, I will ask Mayor Beame and Governor Carey to come to the White House, and I would say: "Look, I'm willing to join you as an equal partner to work out New York City's problems."

And I would try to discern a time schedule during which that could be consummated. It probably would take eight years.

Compulsory Unionism

There are two different right-to-work laws. One is a state law, one is a federal law [Section 14-B of the Taft-Hartley Act]. The federal law gives the state the option whether there will be right-to-work or not.

When I was governor of Georgia I said if repeal [of the right-to-work law] passed the legislature, I'd be prepared to sign it. Now, as a candidate for the presidency, I've said the same thing at the federal level. If 14-B is repealed by Congress, I'll be prepared to sign it into law.

But I'm not going to take on repeal of 14-B as a crusade for myself as president. Why not? Because I don't think it's that important.

Mandatory Busing

Well, in the first place, I don't think we ought to amend the Constitution every time we have a transient problem, and that's what I consider the busing problem to be—transient.

Secondly, in most instances where busing orders have been put forth, the communities have eventually accommodated themselves to a workable procedure. That was the case with Atlanta, with which I am familiar.

Third, I would hate to reopen the entire divisive question of busing for all the state legislatures in the nation to debate again. It would unnecessarily create disharmony, racial and otherwise, if this question was thrust on the nation to decide.

In some instances, mandatory busing has worked relatively well, with small numbers of students involved in the plan.

I've always made it clear I don't favor mandatory busing simply to achieve racial balance.

A Constitutional Amendment on Abortion

I don't think we need to try to change the present ruling of the Supreme Court, though I would prefer a stricter ruling. (Carter also proposed a government program to assist in family planning which, he hopes, would reduce the need for abortions.)

Pardon of Amnesty for Deserters

In the area of the country where I live, defecting from the military service is almost unheard-of. Most of the young people in my section of Georgia are quite poor. They didn't know where Sweden was, they didn't know how to get to Canada, but they didn't have enough money to hide in college.

They thought the war was wrong. They preferred to stay home, but still, they went to Vietnam.

A substantial proportion of them, a substantial disproportion of them, were black. And they've never been recognized for their service to the country. They've often been despised, characterized as criminals—they were never heroes—and I feel a very great appreciation for them.

It's very difficult for me to equate what they did with what the young people did who left the country.

But I think it's time to get the Vietnam war over with. I don't have any desire to punish anyone. I'd just like to tell the young folks who did defect to come back home, with no requirement that you be punished, or that you serve in some humanitarian capacity or anything. Just come back home. The whole thing's over. I'd just issue a blanket pardon, without comment.

His Promise Not to Lie

When I first said it, I didn't anticipate any particular notice of it, because this is the way I deeply felt.

I did feel it was inappropriate for a candidate for the presidency to tell a lie. I've had the feeling in the past that presidents have not lied.

I don't think Truman ever lied. I don't think Eisenhower ever lied.

Lately, there's been a common and accepted practice, stated openly, for some of the presidents to say it's necessary to lie. So I think there's now a lack of trust among the people in what their leaders say.

I try to express clearly my position on every question that's asked me, but I don't set for myself any higher standard than any candidate ought to set.

I can see, in retrospect, and I don't regret it, it was like throwing down a gauntlet, because a lot of reporters scurried around trying to find some instance where I may have made a misleading statement.

I feel I've never lied or misled the voters.

Would I say it again if I were starting all over?

Yes.

Why People Vote for Him

That's a hard question for me to answer. I have a genuine

affinity for, or intimacy with, a wide range of voters. I feel completely at home with black groups, environmental groups, farmers, young people, very conservative businessmen, and so forth.

I think they know it, they feel it.

And I derive from them a very strong, very fervent, very dedicated support.

The Soviet Union

They will continue to pursue their ultimate goal to communism, as was expressed very clearly by Brezhnev at the twenty-fifth Party Congress.

They will continue to push for communism throughout the world and to probe for possibilities for expansion of their system, which I think is a legitimate purpose for them. I think we ought to recognize it and be prepared for it.

Future Angolas

I think we have not had the intimate relationship with the developing nations of the world which are in a state of change, because we haven't paid any attention to them.

We supported the Portuguese as long as we could. We tried to see which one of the factions was most beneficial to us without trying to assess what was best for the Angolan people, or which faction in Angola of the tribal groups was most compatible with the needs of Angola.

We watched for many years while Russia and Cuba got firmly entrenched with the Angolan people. And then there's this last-minute thing in secret—Kissinger and Ford and the CIA decided that we would give them military aid, knowing that neither the American people nor the Congress would support that policy.

I would not have gone in.

Military Balance With Russia

The only trend I can see that disturbs me is in the realm of naval strength.

I think we still have superiority over Russia in the multiplicity of delivery systems for atomic weapons and our ability to defend ourselves.

We are not vulnerable to attack from the Russians except

through weapon deliveries. I think the cumulative strength of our own military forces, plus those of NATO and others, are still superior to those of the Soviet Union.

I think that our vast economic capabilities in agricultural production, electronics, etc., gives us a decided edge and will for the next fifteen years.

I think that we are still superior to Russia, even in the navy, although in the last eight years our number of ships has decreased fifty percent, and theirs has doubled.

I think the trends are in the wrong direction. The navy . . . has a profound impact on our ability to consummate a foreign policy in peacetime, and I think the ability to control the seas in a benevolent way is very important.

We are getting on shaky ground now. We have not reassessed our naval strategy since 1950.

We are still predicating our plans on a guess that the next war is going to be in the Far East. I think that's a mistake in basic premise.

Should the U.S. Spend More or Less on Defense?

I would say about the same. Maybe five percent less. We've had some wrong emphases. I'd like to see our Defense Department changed into a much more effective fighting force within the present budgetary limits.

We are wasting enormous quantities of money.

We've got too many bases overseas: about two thousand.

We've got too many support troops per combat troops—about twice as many as the Soviet Union.

We've got too top heavy a layer of personnel assignments.

We've got more admirals and generals than we had at the end of the Second World War.

I think there are a lot of things we could phase out now.

The Corps of Engineers, for all practical purposes, ought to be gotten out of the dam-building business.

We don't need a Selective Service still intact, five years after we have eliminated the draft.

I would remove all atomic bombs from Korea. We've got 700 atomic weapons in Korea. I see no reason for a single one.

There are a lot of things we could do to make the military more effective in its ability to defend us, and I think this would result in some moderate reduction in overall military needs.

But I would not ever let our country be vulnerable. I believe in a strong defense.

The Far East

What concerns me most . . . is that the Japanese unfortunately, because of their growing distrust of this country and their belief that we've not gotten an adequate consultative relationship with them, equate our concern with them to our concern with maintenance of strength in Korea.

I don't think that ought to be part of the Japanese consciousness.

My commitment to Japan would be total.

I think the people believe we ought to maintain our forces in Japan. There are only about twenty-five thousand there, plus about thirty-five thousand in Korea and Okinawa.

But I would not be rash about withdrawal of troops from South Korea. I'd be very careful about that. I'd make sure the Japanese knew what we were doing. . . . I would make sure they understood my motivations in withdrawing atomic weapons from Korea.

Then I would make sure that in the four or five years when we get our troops in Korea substantially removed, that Korea would still be able to defend itself against North Korea.

The Middle East

Israel has become the victim of apparent uncertainties over the future of U.S. conduct.

I would be more strongly committed to Israel than we have been in the past. One of the things that has caused unnecessary tensions in the Middle East is the contradictory nature of our commitments.

I think the Arab countries would be best served if they knew that our first responsibility is the preservation of the right of the nation of Israel to exist in peace.

The Arabs should know that we want to trade with them,

want to be friends with them, and want to encourage, if possible, viable relationships between the Arabs and Israel.

We are willing, as a last resort, to come in as a trilateral entity on an equal basis, as in the case of the Sinai accord. I thought that was a very notable achievement by Mr. Kissinger and I give him credit for it. I disagree with George Ball that it has to be "all or nothing."

Foreign Policy in General

We don't have any predictable foreign policy in our relationships with the various regions of the world: Europe, South America, Africa. We don't have any predictable foreign policy that I can discern, relating to individual nations.

Our foreign policy of late has been conducted primarily in secret. I don't think that our natural allies, or historical supporters, feel that they have been adequately consulted before we make our foreign policy decisions.

This has exacerbated, I think, normal competition between us and the Common Market European countries, between us and Canada, us and Mexico, us and Japan.

I have spent quite some time in the past several years with leaders in those countries—sometimes prime ministers, sometimes foreign ministers, trade ministers, and the like—and they feel left out.

Overseas Commerce

The biggest problem that I have ever had [in my own peanut business] has been with the government. I never know where to go to get an answer to a question: the Export-Import Bank, the Agriculture Department, the State Department, the Defense Department? . . .

Things have got to be made easier and more rational for our exporters.

Another thing: I would remove the incentives that have been built into our own government policies that encourage corporations to manufacture their products in other countries, while their employees here are out of work.

Other countries don't do this.

Speaking during the primary campaign in Abilene, Texas,

Carter was interrupted by an impatient questioner who asked him to sum up what the total aim of his administration's policy would be. Without a moment's hesitation, Carter, quoting from Reinhold Niebuhr, replied: "To establish justice in a sinful world."

8

THE TEACHER

Jimmy is a Bible scholar and a very fine preacher.

—Clarence Dodson

At ten o'clock on Sunday morning, March 28, 1976, twelve men gathered in the upper room of the Baptist Church in Plains, Georgia, to hear a Sunday school lesson on the second coming of Jesus Christ. The teacher was a substitute, the result of a change late the night before and not previously announced. Neither the regular teacher, Clarence Dodson, nor any one else had thought it necessary to spread the word of the change. The members were certain to be there anyway.

The substitute, a fifty-one-year-old member of the Sunday school, a local man with a reputation as a Bible scholar, was former Governor Jimmy Carter, just back from his first real majority victory in the North Carolina presidential primary. He was home for the weekend before heading again into one of his toughest, closest battles for presidential support, in Wisconsin.

Dressed in a blue seersucker suit, a blue shirt, and a red tie, the substitute teacher took his place behind a small, round table under a single, bare light bulb. The walls of the room were stark white. He began with a question:

"Suppose you were informed this afternoon that Jesus was to come tonight and you had just five hours to live; what would you do to get ready for the presence of Christ?"

He paused. "You might think of all the people you had hurt, or of those for whom you had some hatred in your heart, and you might get on the phone and say: 'Look, I'm sorry.'

"You might talk to your wife about something you had said to her. You might think of something you had never admitted you had done, or of something you hadn't been able to carry out, or someone you had intended to witness to about Jesus, who had not known him. And you might say to him, 'let me tell you about Christ dying on the cross.'

"But those things we would do in the five hours are the things we should be doing this afternoon. We should live our lives as though Christ were going to come this afternoon, so we would be prepared when he put out his hand, and said: 'Frank, or Clarence, or Hugh, here we are together.' "

He paused, and then went on.

"No, Jesus hasn't told us when he is coming, but we should be ready. And if there is something in our lives that we should change, let's do it."

It was a relaxed, friendly group of men, most of them in their forties or fifties, and they listened intently to Carter's hour-long discourse on the twenty-fourth chapter of Matthew—a passage that deals with both the second coming and the destruction of the temple of Jerusalem.

Among the class members were State Senator Hugh Carter, Jimmy's first cousin; Frank Williams, Carter's chief competitor in the Georgia peanut business; Dale Gay, a contractor with the Home Construction Company of Americus; Ralph Speegle, a dairyman; and Cody Timmerman, a retired railroad engineer. There were also a mail carrier, a hospital employee, a business manager, and one federal worker.

Turning to his Bible to read about the destruction of the temple, Carter said he had often wondered about the "great mystery" of the destruction of the temple. He found it "a bit confusing," he said.

"Last Sunday, we saw that the Pharisees were asking Christ questions, trying to trip him up. He challenged them, and told them they were a generation of vipers, who ignored the general teachings of God.

"Now this was the week before Jesus died," Carter reminded the class, "and after that encounter with the Pharisees there was no doubt in the minds of his disciples that he was going to be crucified.

"The last Tuesday of his life he went into the temple."

Then, folding the Bible over a place-marker for a moment, the presidential candidate recalled his own visit to Jerusalem.

"Rosalynn and I have been in old Jerusalem," he said. "We were there for three or four days, and we would get up at daybreak and walk in the old city with maps and try to figure out where different places were that Jesus had gone. And we saw the temple site.

"In Christ's time, it had been the third temple built. The second one was built about 516 B.C. The third temple was built by Herod. It was small, compared to what Herod wanted. But it was sturdy, and some of the stones were eighteen feet thick. Some of them were as big as a house."

Turning again to his Bible, he went on:

"As Christ and his disciples were leaving the temple, they went up in the hills to spend a night, and the disciples were saying that the temple would last till eternity. But Jesus replied, 'Not a stone will be left standing.'

"When they got to the Mount of Olives, the disciples asked him what he meant. They were all sure about this time that his life was going to be over because they had had a premonition about it. There was a building hatred against him.

"Jesus told them the temple was going to be destroyed and he went on to tell them that the other Jerusalem would be at the coming of the judgment . . . and that is the purpose of the lesson this morning."

Looking up, again, from his Bible and peering straight into the eyes of the class members, Carter put the rest of the lesson entirely in his own words.

"Jesus stands at the door and knocks, but he won't break down the door. He doesn't want to. It must be opened by our understanding. It must be self-willed.

"And his word has to be carried on by those of us who love him. If we don't carry it on, it won't be carried on at all. We are the Johns and Peters and Matthews and Pauls."

Then, in a final word as he closed his Bible, the substitute teacher spoke softly:

"The main point I want to leave with you today is that we should lead our lives with the Holy Spirit within us, and be ready to face our Savior. We should leave here today and live our lives as though Jesus were coming this afternoon."

Then the bell rang for the eleven o'clock preaching service.

Jimmy Carter's activities in behalf of the Plains Baptist Church's Sunday school program span several decades. The older members of the church recall with a chuckle how Jimmy, at the age of eleven or twelve, would borrow his mother's old, black Plymouth and drive all around the countryside rounding up little boys who didn't have a way to get to Sunday school.

"He was so tiny he could barely see over the steering wheel," recalled Anne Dodson, who has known Jimmy for over forty years. "I'll never forget the sight of all those little boys piling out of that car at the church on Sunday mornings."

Her husband, Clarence, the regular teacher of the men's class, talked freely about his substitute. "He comes to class every Sunday he's home," he said. "But he only teaches if he has time to do the study. Then he'll call me and ask me if he can fill in for me. He teaches about every six weeks. He called me last night about eleven o'clock and said, 'Clarence, would you mind if I taught your class tomorrow?' I'm always delighted."

Not just everybody is allowed to teach in the Bible classes of the church, Dodson said. "They have to be active members of the church, members of the Bible class, and they have to have taken training at special Bible courses, and know the Bible extremely well."

"Jimmy," he added, "is a Bible scholar and a very fine preacher."

Other neighbors recall that Carter taught a class of very young girls while he was a student at Annapolis. Back in Plains, he took over a Sunday school class of elementary school boys. And he taught in Sunday school in Atlanta throughout his term as governor.

Carter and his wife, Rosalynn, who had attended another Sunday school class downstairs, took seats in the third row of pews for the church service. They shared a hymnal and both of them sang. Carter joined in the prayer, with his head in his hands, occasionally nodding agreement, as the pastor, the Reverend Bruce Edwards, prayed that they all turn away from their tendencies to "trust themselves and to lean on their own ability and intellect."

Afterward, on the steps of the seventy-year-old white church, the Carters chatted with members of the congregation, most of whom they had known throughout their lives. Then they went home to pack the candidate's bags for the trip to Wisconsin.

9

CHRISTIANITY AND
THE PRESIDENCY

I don't look on the presidency as a pastorate . . . No. Although Teddy Roosevelt said it's a bully pulpit, no, I don't look on it with religious connotations. But it gives me a chance to serve, and it also gives me a chance to magnify whatever influence I have, for either good or bad, and I hope it will be for good.

—Jimmy Carter

Weary from a long day of campaigning, Carter sank deep into the cushioned comfort of an elegant living room in exclusive Georgetown, along the Potomac River, in Washington. He had gone to the home of Ward Chamberlin, president of Washington's public television station, WETA, to talk awhile about God and the role that his faith in Christ played in his life. Sitting with him, in a brief respite from the crowds and the clamor, was forty-two-year-old Bill D. Moyers, the former "boy wonder" of the administration of President Lyndon B. Johnson.

"The fact that a person has deep religious convictions," he explained to Moyers, "does not necessarily mean that that person thinks he's always right, or that God has ordained him to take a dominant position."

Then, after a pause, he added: "Although I have prayed a good bit—and do—I've never asked God to let me be president."

"What do you pray for then?" Moyers asked.

"Well, I ask God to let me do what's right, and let me do what's best, that my life be meaningful, in an optimum way, and if I win or lose I believe I can accept the decision with composure and without regrets or animosities, or hatreds or even deep disappointment."

This was not just a chance meeting. The two of them had been brought together to see if they could, between them, put into words a clear picture of the kind of faith that moves an ambitious politician to tell the voters, in a crucial election year, that Jesus Christ, not the presidency, comes first in his priorities.

It was April 15, 1976, and Carter had come close to defeat in the Wisconsin primary, only a week before. His slender winning margin did not appear until the early morning hours the day after the election.

And less than two weeks ahead was the crucial Pennsylvania primary election, an election in a major industrial state that had the added disadvantage—for Carter—of a hostile boss rule in its major center of voting strength, Philadelphia.

Even worse, the Carter campaign chest was almost empty.

So, as he talked to President Johnson's former colleague, the thoughts that passed through Carter's mind were not, in the natural, reassuring.

Floodlights were temporarily ranged around the room as they talked. And a heavy television camera left deep indentations in the carpeting as it silently recorded the scene and the words from an unobtrusive corner just in front of the two men.

Moyers—now one of the country's top broadcasters and journalists—seemed ideal for the assignment. Not only is he himself a Southern Baptist; he also is a graduate of a Southern Baptist seminary. And, as Carter had in 1976, Moyers had had a meteoric political rise in the sixties. At the age of only twenty-nine, in 1963, he had risen to be special assistant to President Johnson and later to be presidential press secretary, a job that capped his four years in the White House hierarchy. Among all the journalists on the national scene he seemed the most likely to ask the right questions about religious matters, and the most likely man to understand the answers.

"Do you ever have any doubts?" he asked. "People say to me—'Jimmy Carter seems to be so full of certainty, and conviction, in a time when, as Gabriel said in *Green Pastures*, "everything that's tied together is coming loose." ' Do you have any doubts about yourself, about God, about life?"

"I can't think of any," Carter said, with a slight shake of the head. Then he went on:

"I obviously don't know all the answers to philosophical questions and theological questions—the kind of questions that are contrived. But the things that I haven't been able to answer, in theory or supposition, I just accept them and go on—things that I can't influence or change.

"But doubt about my faith? No.

"Doubt about my purpose of life? I don't have any doubts about that."

Moyers recalled that Carter had once said in a public speech that his religious life had been significantly influenced by a sermon he had heard, entitled: "If You Were Arrested for Being a Christian, Would There Be Enough Evidence to Convict You?"

"What is the evidence that the rest of us can see of a Christian?"

There was a long pause before the answer came.

"That's a hard question to answer, because I don't think I'm better than anyone else. I recognize my own shortcomings and sinfulness and my need to improve, and the need for forgiveness from the people around me, and from God.

"I was going through a stage in my life that was a very difficult one. I had run for governor and lost. Nothing I did was gratifying. When I succeeded in something I got no pleasure out of it. When I failed at something, it was a horrible experience for me.

"I thought I was a good Christian. I was chairman of the board of deacons; I was the head of the brotherhood in all of the thirty-four churches in my district, and head of the finance committee, and a Sunday school teacher just about all of my life.

"Then one day the preacher gave this sermon. I don't remember a thing he said. I just remember the title that you just described—'If You Were Arrested for Being a Christian, Would There Be Enough Evidence to Convict You?'

"And my answer by the time the sermon was over was 'No.'

"I never had really committed myself totally to God. My Christian beliefs were superficial. They were based primarily on pride. I never had done much for other people. I was always thinking about myself.

"So I changed somewhat for the better. I formed a much more intimate relationship with Christ. And since then I've had just about a new life. As far as hatreds, frustrations—I feel at ease with myself. Now that doesn't mean I'm better, but I'm better off myself."

Then another question was put: "How do you know—this is a question I hear from a lot of people—how do you know God's will?"

"Well, I pray frequently—not continually, but many times a day. When I have a sense of peace and self-assurance—I don't know where it comes from—what I'm doing is a right thing, I assume, maybe in an unwarranted way, that that's doing God's will."

Again, a question from Moyers: "What do you think we are on earth for?"

"I don't know. You know I could quote Bible references, through creation, that God created us in his own image, hoping that we'd be perfect. But we turned out not to be perfect, but very sinful, and then when Jesus was asked what were the great commandments from God which should direct our lives, he said to love God with all your heart and soul and mind, and love your neighbor as yourself.

"So I try to take that summary of Christian theology and let it be something through which I search for a meaningful existence. I don't worry about it too much anymore. I used to when I was a college sophomore, and we used to debate for hours and hours why we are here, who made us, where we should go, what's our purpose.

"But I don't feel frustrated about it. I'm not afraid to see my life ended, I feel like every day is meaningful. I don't have any fear at all of death. I feel like I'm doing the best I can, and if I get elected president, I'll have a chance to magnify my own influence, maybe in a beneficial way. If I don't get elected president, I'll go back to Plains.

"So I feel I have a sense of equanimity about it. But why we're here on earth I don't know. . . ."

"What drives you?" the questioner asked.

"I don't know exactly how to express it. As I have said, it's not an unpleasant sense of being driven. I feel like I have one life to live—I feel that God wants me to do the best I can with it. And that's quite often my major prayer—let me live my life so that it will be meaningful. And I enjoy tackling difficult problems, and solving them. And I enjoy the meticulous organization of a complicated effort. It's a challenge. Possibly it's like a game. I don't know. I don't want to lower it by saying it's just a game—but it's an enjoyable thing for me."

Turning then to the subject of compromise and how a need to compromise might lead to dangers, the questioner put this:

"I think what some people in this town [Washington] are talking about is the unwillingness of a Woodrow Wilson to compromise on the League of Nations, the unwillingness of Lyndon Johnson to compromise on the war, and there is a feeling that a disciplined, principled man, convinced of his own rightness, or having a private pipeline to God, in a sense, is going to say: 'I'm right.' And the town won't function because of his inability to compromise. Is that a legitimate danger?"

91

"I don't believe so," Carter replied quickly. "I can see that that would be a legitimate concern, but I think the concern will be proven to be unjustified. They have a right to be concerned, but I don't think they need to be.

"I'd like to quote one other thing—you've gotten into theology—Tillich said that religion is a search for the relationship between us and God, and us and our fellow human beings. And he went on to say that when we quit searching, in effect, we've lost our religion. When we become self-satisfied, proud, sure—at that point we lose the self-searching, the humility, the subservience to God's will, the intimate understanding of other people's needs, and the mere inclination to be accommodating, and in that instant, we lose our religion."

Moyers: "In your own search for what Tillich said is the truth about man's relationship to man and to God, what's the most significant discovery Jimmy Carter has made?"

"Well, I think I described it superficially a while ago. I think it affected my life more than anything else. This is embarrassing a little bit for me to talk about, because it's personal, but in my relationship with Christ, and with God, I became able in the process to look at it in practical terms, to accept defeat, to get pleasure out of successes, to be at peace with the world.

"For instance, one of the things I derived from it, again in a kind of embarrassing way, when I stand out on a factory shift line like I did this morning [the General Electric plant in Erie, Pennsylvania]—everybody that comes through there, when I shake hands with them, for that instant, I really care about them in a genuine way.

"And I believe they know it a lot of times. Quite often I will shake hands with women who work in a plant, and I just touch their hands and, not infrequently, they'll put their arms around my neck and say, 'God bless you, son,' or 'good luck, I'll help you.'

"But it's a kind of relationship with the people around me, but I don't want to insinuate that I'm better than other people. I've still got a long way to go. But you asked me a difficult question: What was the major discovery of my life? That's a hard thing to answer."

"But you care, though?"

"I care."

"You have found that you care about people?"

"I do."

"Then why not be a pastor or a bishop instead of president?"

"You've read my book," Mr. Carter replied, laughing. "This came up early in my life, when I got home from the navy, and I was thinking about running for the Georgia Senate.

"Some of your viewers haven't read the book. And we had a visiting pastor, and he was giving me a hard time about going into politics. He said it was a disgraceful profession—stay out of it. And I got angry, and I turned to him and kind of lashed back and said: 'How would you like to be pastor of a church with 80,000 members?'—because there were 80,000 people in this state senate district. I don't look on the presidency as a pastorate."

Moyers: "I was going to ask you if the president was a pastor of 230 million? . . ."

Carter: "No. Although Teddy Roosevelt said it's a bully pulpit, no, I don't look on it with religious connotations. But it gives me a chance to serve, and it also gives me a chance to magnify whatever influence I have, for either good or bad, and I hope it will be for good."

Moyers recalled that some political writers had discerned a "ruthless" streak in Carter, despite his smile and his professions of love for the human race. He quoted one writer who said: "In a ruthless business, Mr. Carter is a ruthless operator, even as he wears his broad smile and displays his southern charm."

"And the question arises," Moyers said. "I've been inside the White House and I know some of the influences that work on a man trying to do the right things—can you be ruthless in the way I think it means here, and remain a Christian?"

Carter: "I'm a Christian, no matter what."

Moyers: "How do you reconcile?"

Carter: "He was talking about the campaign, and I don't know what he meant by 'ruthless.' I don't think I've ever deliberately hurt one of my opponents, to gain an advantage. I try not to. I don't remember when I have. There may have been something I've said in the heat of competition that made them feel discomforted. I can't deny that. But most people, when they get to know me, have finally decided that I'm much tougher than is originally apparent.

"The word 'ruthless' to me has connotations of cruelty. And I'm not sure I could be cruel. But I think I can be tough in making difficult decisions. And I can be tenacious under difficult circumstances.

"One of the major criticisms of me, by my opponents in the legislature, who've never yet been assuaged, is that I can't compromise. That's a common criticism. I often had to compromise, but I didn't compromise in a back room. And I didn't compromise to begin with. My purpose was to spread out my position openly—this is what I propose. These are the reasons for it. This is the mess we have now. This is what we can accomplish. Try to work harmoniously with the legislature. Try to give them all the credit they could, and then fight to the last vote.

"I was never much able to fit into a back room and compromise things away that I believed in. And that's a very legitimate source of criticism of me. I'm not a good compromiser. But I don't think Georgia suffered under my administration because of that attitude."

Moyers: "What do you want for your children that you didn't have?"

Carter: "Well, I have to say that I had almost everything that I needed. I worked hard when I was a little child, but I'm proud of it. I didn't travel much when I was a little child, but I don't regret it now. I think those travels through the fields and swamps were, in retrospect, very precious days for me.

"So, I would like to see what they already have—a much

greater awareness of the world structure. My eight-year-old daughter now knows more about biology and science and history and politics and foreign affairs than I did when I went off to college. And it's because she has television, because she reads constantly, and because we educate her well.

"And you know, we focus into her what we have learned. So each generation has a chance to be better, as far as knowledge is concerned. But, also, they've lost something."

Moyers: "Lost something?"

Carter: "Did I mention earlier, I think I did, that I had a stability there? You know, when things started going wrong in my own life, my mother and father were there; and the church was there—which never did change, never has changed yet—but there was something there around which I built my life.

"In the modern-day world, you don't have that. It's a mobile world, and things to cling to are kind of scarce, and few and far between. And which one of those advantages and disadvantages is the greater? I don't know.

"I wouldn't swap the life I had for the new, modern, fast-moving, open, nonstructured, minimal family life, but there are advantages now, I know: more and earlier traveling, having a tighter inter-relationship with your own peer group than I had. But which is better? I don't know.

"But maybe we could go back to some of those old principles that we knew when we went to the B.Y.P.U. [Baptist Young People's Union] on Sunday afternoon, and at the same time keep the advantages of a modern world. I'm sure we can keep the advantages of the modern world, but going back to those principles that give stability, they are things that we're still searching for. We haven't found them yet."

Moyers: "Do you need power?"

Carter: "Oh, I don't think so. That is, an unfulfilled all-obsessive hunger? No. I feel powerful enough now. Secure enough now, and wealthy enough now. I have a good family life now. There are a lot of blessings that would give me a good life for the rest of my days. But I'd like to have a chance to change things that I don't like, and to correct inequities as I discern them, and to be a strong spokesman for those who are not strong, and I guess that's a commensurate part of power. I can't deny that one of my purposes in wanting to be president is power. Yes."

Moyers: "If we've learned anything in the last few years it has been that good intentions in the use of great power is no guarantee that that power will be used wisely."

Carter: "That's right."

Moyers: "But the character of the man is less important to the safeguards against the abuse of power than the checks-and-balances on the office and on the power."

Carter: "I understand that."

Moyers: "And here is Jimmy Carter coming along, saying, 'I want to do all these things because I believe they are right. I want more power because I want to do good things. And trust me. I won't abuse the power.'

"Now after these last ten years, why should someone believe you? They may trust you. They may know that you are sincere, and well-intentioned. Yet they know that it is power that often changes the man and not the man who changes the power."

Carter: "I know. I can see that. That's why I go back to what I said originally. We need to have an open government. We need to tell the truth. A minimum of secrecy, so the people will have a maximum part to play in the evolution and the consummation of our domestic and foreign policies.

"That gives you a safety net under an incompetent or distorted president—the people themselves. I think if we had told the people the truth about Vietnam, we would have been out very early. If the people had had the truth about Watergate, it would never have happened."

Moyers: "So you're saying Jimmy Carter's character is not enough?"

Carter: "That's right."

Moyers: "You want checks. You want balances. You want safeguards?"

Carter: "I don't object to those. I don't object to a strong, aggressive Congress. And a strong, aggressive Supreme Court, and a strong aggressive president—if what goes on in our government is known by, debated by, questioned by, controlled by the people of this country.

"Now I can see that there are times when an inspirational leader can actually elevate the people. That may happen on a rare occasion. I think for a time, at least, John Kennedy did it. Roosevelt did it. This is part of the presidency.

"There are times when the presidency, perhaps the government itself, might tend to sink below the standards of the people of this country. In which case, the people support, or boost that official, or those officials, in a weak moment. But to exclude the people completely, as we have tended to do in recent years, that removes that common sense, judgment, character, safety that can preserve our country.

"And it also destroys the concept of our government, which is that the government ought to be controlled by the people, and not by a powerful, secret, hidden, isolated, mistaken president.

"I don't want to see that ever happen again in this country.

"I'd like to set the kind of tone—and perhaps the kinds of laws—that would prevent a recurrence of these things, if that's humanly possible."

Moyers: "You are saying, in effect, then: 'Trust me and I will do these things'?"

Carter: "Yes."

10

ROSALYNN

We need your help, so that with your help and the help of our Lord Jesus Christ, Jimmy Carter can be a great president of these United States.

—Rosalynn Carter

It was Sunday, two days before the hard-fought Maryland primary election. Mrs. Jimmy Carter—Rosalynn—had been campaigning for her husband since dawn. This was her last stop before lunch.

The pastor of the all-black Gillies Memorial Community Church in Baltimore, the Reverend Theodore Jackson, was introducing her and giving her husband a resounding endorsement in his race for the presidency. Looking slim and pretty and a decade younger than her forty-eight years, she moved to the pulpit and began her own endorsement of her husband of thirty years.

"It is pleasant to be here with you this morning and to join you in praising the Lord, and to have the opportunity to say a few words about my husband, Jimmy Carter, who is running for president," she began in soft, Georgian tones.

"In his inaugural address as governor of Georgia he said: 'The time for racial discrimination is over. No longer shall any poor, weak or black person be deprived of the opportunity of an education, a job or simple justice.' "

The congregation responded with a wave of "amens."

"He felt a real responsibility for those people in our state who are affected by government," she went on. "He lived up to this responsibility. You know if you are wealthy you don't need so many of these services. The wealthy can send their children to private schools. They don't have to worry about the Health Department or the Welfare Department."

There was chorus of "yes, yes," from the listeners.

"I wish I had time to tell you of all the things he did," she said. "We had one of the worst systems of government in this nation in Georgia. At the end of four years we had one of the best systems of government. I, myself, worked with the Health Department of our state. We had one of the worst. Now we have one of the best. That is why I say it was a gratifying experience for me.

"We looked around, and there were no portraits in the capitol of our great black leaders. So we put up the portraits of Martin Luther King, Jr., and others."

More "amens" from the congregation, and she continued: "My husband deputized all high school principals as voter registrars to see that every high school student was registered to vote before he reached the age of eighteen.

"Dr. Martin Luther King, Sr., is my good friend," she continued, as the audience nodded and there was an undertone of approving comments. "The day his wife was shot in his church, Jimmy was in a Democratic telethon in California, so I went to his house to be with him through that time.

"I was in his church the last Sunday he preached in his own church. He'll never stop preaching. And he told me that day that he thought my husband would be a great president and that he was with him all the way."

Another "amen" chorus.

"Another thing I want you to know about my husband is that he's a Christian man. He has told me many times that he spent more time on his knees, as governor of Georgia, than in all the rest of his life put together.

"We need your help, so that with your help and the help of our Lord Jesus Christ, Jimmy Carter can be a great president of these United States."

As the petite southern lady left the pulpit it occurred to a lone white man sitting near the rear of the church that that was one of the most undebatable, unanswerable political speeches he had heard in his half-century career of listening to and writing about politicians.

It was one-thirty in the afternoon when Rosalynn stopped for lunch in one of the all-black neighborhoods of Baltimore after her three church appearances that morning. She spoke freely throughout the meal about her husband, his candidacy, and his faith.

On one of their rare weekends at home together in Plains, she said, she asked Jimmy what would happen if he lost the race for the presidency. "He said he'd go out in the backyard—we live on the edge of the woods—and say a prayer, and then go down to the warehouse and go to work."

She laughed as she recalled the incident, but she said, like her husband, that she is certain that it was God's will that he make a try for the presidency. And she revealed the same sort of confidence of the outcome that the candidate himself showed throughout the campaign.

"You feel encouraged, of course, by the way your husband's campaign is going, but," she was asked, "do you think sometimes that this success may be some sort of a sign that you are, indeed, doing God's will? Do you think that, in spite of the well-known fact your husband's campaign is being run by a roster of amateurs and novices—which might be considered quite a handicap—his success might be a sign that somebody higher up is really in charge?"

Mrs. Carter bristled slightly at the demeaning remarks about the close-knit group of joyful youngsters who make up ninety percent of the Carter team. But she hastened to point out that "most of our staff are people who worked with us the whole time Jimmy was governor.

"We didn't have the money, we couldn't afford to get the experts in the various fields," she said. "We just couldn't afford it.

"His executive secretary while he was governor [Hamilton Jordan, thirty-one], a young man who has helped us the whole time he has run for office, was his campaign manager then, and he is his campaign manager now.

"His press secretary [Jody Powell, thirty-two], who has been with us from the time Jimmy was running for governor, was going to Emory, and he came and knocked on the door and wanted to help in the campaign. He was press secretary while he was governor, and he's press secretary in this national campaign. They were people whose backgrounds we knew.

"I don't know about signs.

"I know that we pray daily for guidance.

"I, for instance, had never made speeches until Jimmy was governor. I didn't think that I could do anything like that. Then somebody sent me this little tract that's titled: 'Lovingly in the Hands of the Father.' It says that if you put yourself at all times 'lovingly in the hands of the Father,' he takes care of you all the time, and you can do anything you have to do.

"So I found I could get up and stand in front of those crowds of people, and think to myself 'I'm lovingly in the hands of the Father,' and I do it.

"I think Jimmy does the same thing.

"One day, I remember, I told him I was worried about what I was saying in the radio interviews. I was afraid I might say something that would hurt, something that would not be the way he would answer it.

"He said: 'Don't you pray before you go on radio? Don't you pray if you know you're going to be on the radio? Don't you say 'God help me, God help me'?

"I told him 'yes.'

" 'Well, that's all that's necessary,' he said. 'Just ask the

Lord to help you do the best you can. And you'll do all right.'

"I know that's the way he does it. He does the best job that he possibly can do, then he just turns it over to the Lord. That's all he can do."

"But does your husband ever find that, because his young staff members may not be thinking or acting on the same wavelength with him—since they may not be so fully committed to the Lord—that there are frequent misunderstandings, difficulties or disagreements?" she was asked.

"I don't really know. Maybe, sometimes, on how to run the campaign. But Jimmy directs it. He has a campaign manager, but Jimmy has the final word about what to do. The positions that Jimmy takes are his own. But that's something you'll have to ask him about."

Mrs. Carter was asked: "What makes your husband think that a dedicated Christian can be a successful president of all the people—and that includes the Jews and all the other non-Christians, plus all the millions who are nominal Christians and frequently talk and act like something quite different?"

"I think he believes that if he turns to God in prayer before he makes decisions that he will make the right decisions about the way things affect the lives of people of our country," she replied.

"He was a good governor, and as governor he saw no conflict between his religion and the government. And there are so many ways to serve in the position of governor and the position of president.

"There are so many different types of people in the country. But with God's guidance I think he believes he can take care of all those types of situations."

Thinking back for a moment to their experience in the governor's mansion in Georgia, Mrs. Carter recalled that "we tried to work with Lester Maddox as lieutenant governor, because it was going to be that way for the next four years. There's no telling what Jimmy could have done as governor if he'd had a cooperative lieutenant governor. But it didn't last even until inauguration day."

"Will religion be a factor in his appointments as president?" Rosalynn was asked. "Has he ever discussed this with you?"

"No, he has never discussed it with me, but I am sure it will be."

"In what way?"

"In looking into their backgrounds, for instance, he will check not only to see that they are qualified for the job, but that they are also honest, respectable people. And I am sure he will ask God for guidance."

11

THE CRITICS

I want to be tested in the most severe way. I want the American people to understand my character and my weaknesses, the kind of person I am.

—Jimmy Carter

"Why do they hate him?" The question came from a relaxed and reclining aide of Jimmy Carter, his stocking-clad feet propped high on the back of a seat in the candidate's campaign plane, his tie loosened and his shirt sleeves folded back halfway to the elbows.

Piled beside him in disarray was a heap of discarded newspapers gathered from cities in many parts of the country. And on the floor and under surrounding seats was a scattering of bits and pieces of clipped—but usually torn—pages of newsprint that had yielded stories he thought "the governor" might like to see.

"Just listen to this," he said, picking up the torn-out fragment of a page. "This guy is described as an 'aide to Morris Udall,' and listen to what he tells this reporter: 'I'll never support Carter. I'd rather vote for Ford. Carter's so damn

104

slick. What monopoly does he have on goodness? To me, he's dangerous.'

"Now does that make sense to you?" the aide asked, looking up. "He hates the governor because he uses the word 'God' so often, and because he admits that he prays for guidance before he makes a major decision. Now I ask you, is that a legitimate reason for attacking a man?"

The indignant staffer shook his head in disbelief, and, without waiting for an answer, reached for the next paper and opened it.

To the listener, who had been standing in the aisle of the plane to get the cramps out of his legs, it occurred that Carter might be less surprised and outraged than his helper. As a student of the Bible, the governor might immediately spot this comment as one of the oldest reasons in the book for hating him—a reason almost two thousand years old. Even one with only a Sunday school recollection of the Scriptures might recognize in it a fulfillment of words Christ spoke to the multitudes in the Sermon on the Mount: "Blessed are ye, when men shall revile you, and persecute you, and shall say all manner of evil against you falsely, for my sake."

But others would offer different explanations.

Alan Baron, Senator George McGovern's press secretary, for example, pounced on Carter's promise that he would never lie. With undertones of knowing sarcasm, he told a reporter: "By saying that he would never tell a lie, Carter decided for himself that that's going to be his standard. Well, fine, let's hold him to it." They're still listening for that first lie.

Governor George Wallace of Alabama complained bitterly that Carter had promised to support him for president in 1972 and then reneged. Carter's reply to this frequently repeated charge was that the letter in which he told Governor Wallace that he would not support him was in the Georgia state archives and available to any who wanted the facts behind his refusal.

McGovern himself rejected all suggestions that he support Carter, on grounds that the former Georgia governor joined forces with those who tried to stop the senator's nomination at the convention in 1972. Carter had this half-serious comment: "I had hoped George would remember the golden rule."

One former governor of a northern state made it clear that success not only bred more success, but also tended to surround the successful one with nit-picking jealousy. "It was obvious that he [Carter] was a hustler," he recalled of his associations with Carter in the governors conference. "His style was just a little different: soft voice, soft sell. But there was a political road map all over his face. Jimmy would take advantage of any single opportunity to further himself. He is absolutely driven."

Then, this same former governor added, somewhat grudgingly, "But unlike a lot of politicians, he knows who he is and where he wants to go."

Senator Wendell Ford of Kentucky, also a former governor, told a reporter, "I don't know of any governors or former governors whom Carter has contacted for support. That might indicate how much support he has among his former colleagues."

The Carter camp acknowledged that support of the nation's governors had been "dampened"—to put it mildly—by Carter's declaration that as president he would propose that federal revenue-sharing money be sent directly to the mayors of cities and not to the state governors. The mayors, he said, are closer to the real needs of the people than the governors and more likely to use the money wisely.

The left wing of the Democratic party almost literally went into shock when Carter turned out to be the winner in New Hampshire, instead of its favorite, Udall. "We think we have good reason to suspect," one commented, "that this independent stance of his may be just a camouflage for a 'closet conservative.' "

Carter also had no record as a part of the "old-boy liberal network," although his liberalism was considered downright radical by his opponents in Georgia. Liberals of the northeastern states held anguished meetings, after New Hampshire, on "what to do about Carter." Many of them eventually came up with an answer: "Vote for him."

Joseph Duffey, director of the American Association of University Professors, offered a combination of learned and down-to-earth analysis of the fearful puzzlement over Carter among the northeastern liberals. "The anti-Carter sentiment," he said, "is the cultural provincialism of a group that finds it hard to relate to someone who is neither a knee-jerk liberal nor an ideologue."

Mark Shields, a Washington-based political consultant often involved in Democratic campaigns, put it in plainer language: "The problem is that no one in Washington feels that they own a piece of Jimmy Carter."

Carter himself analyzed the distrust and hatred that had been leveled at him in this way: "I have been accused of being an outsider. I plead guilty. Unfortunately—or fortunately, for me—the vast majority of Americans also are outsiders.

"We are not going to get changes by simply shifting around the same groups of insiders, the same tired old rhetoric, the same unkept promises and the same divisive appeals to one party, one faction, one section of the country, one race or religion, or one interest group. The insiders have had their chances, and they have not delivered. Their time has run out."

One of the motives for the continuing attacks on Carter was generally left unstated in the press and was stated only in whispers in conversations. It was this: Carter is a proud southern gentleman, who earned the title "gentleman" and did not inherit it along with family wealth. He comes from a section of the South that is most suspect among the northern liberals in the Democratic party and he has been known to boast of his origin as a "redneck" son of the hard-baked red Georgia soil, while denying any and all racial connotations of that boast.

Beyond that, he is also an earnest Southern Baptist who openly admits that his faith in Jesus Christ is the most important thing in his life. And his southern style of evangelistic speech-making, which filters through into so many of his political speeches, irritated many of the less zealous Christians in his northern audiences.

On the other hand, this style did attract large numbers of the country's legion of evangelical Christians to his banner. And it frequently attracted some already high in the ranks of governing officials. For example, Governor Dolph Briscoe of Texas went to a Carter rally in the spring of 1976 as a friendly, but uncommitted Democrat. As he left the rally he was approached by a group of reporters. They asked him what he thought of this new southern candidate. "I like Jimmy Carter because he's a Christian," the governor told them. "I'm going to support him."

Carter said that, as governor of Georgia, he regarded his new social programs as "an extension of the gospel—problem-solving combined with Christian charity."

He frequently referred to this phase of his official work as part of his "Christian ministry to the suffering," and he said he was thankful that he had managed to give to the poor without overly offending the well-to-do and to conquer the opposition to his programs without excessively dividing the legislature and his own party.

More and more, the most important issue of the '76 campaign was Carter's character and personality. Contributing to this possibly was a shortcoming that those around him professed to see, but which Carter was not known to acknowledge himself. That shortcoming, as stated by his own campaign manager, Hamilton Jordan, was this:

"In spite of his earnest emphasis on establishing an intimate relationship with the voters, the governor is not easy to get close to. He doesn't have enough time in his life to let people get close. He doesn't really understand the personal element in politics, though nobody is better at campaigning."

It was during his days as governor that he developed his distaste for wasting time. He found that his time was limited and that he could not do all the things he wanted to do if he allowed persons less urgently occupied to take up his time. So, according to his press secretary, Jody Powell, the governor developed his own system of eliminating time-wasting interruptions.

"If he can't get rid of the people he believes are wasting his time, he simply leaves the room himself—not physically, but mentally," Powell said. "He just turns the whole thing off and puts his mind to work on something else that he believes is more productive."

The governor conceded that this was true and acknowledged that it might be one reason why many people had developed a keen dislike for him; they sometimes felt, quite correctly, that he was not listening to them.

"There's a lot I want to do, and I have just so much time to do it in, and I don't like to waste any time at all on anything that I don't believe is important," he said.

When he was governor, and later as a national leader, Carter often—right in the midst of a conference or conversation—closed his eyes, put his fist under his chin, bowed his head slightly, and talked to the Lord for a few seconds while the conversation continued around him. Visitors often misinterpreted this as a sign of fatigue, and came away with stories that "the governor is working too hard." But for Carter it was part of a lifelong habit of seeking the Lord's guidance "on the spot," while issues were being discussed and before any irreversible decisions were made.

Furthermore, when he believed he had received guidance as to the right thing to do, he was inclined to get testy if the practicalities of life or the campaign prevented him from doing it right away. For example, when the total of delegates committed to him reached about a thousand, Carter felt, very strongly, that the right thing to do, at that moment, was to transfer more of his time to the job of unifying the Democratic party and making peace with those who had been opposing him. He was also impatient to start the planning of the fall campaign, and even the planning for the early days of the Carter administration.

So it was an irritation to him—an irritation that showed through publicly on occasions—that he was forced instead to keep on proving himself to the party leaders and the public.

Otherwise, Carter said he welcomed the ordeal of the primaries, press coverage and all, because "I want to be tested in the most severe way.

"I want the American people to understand my character and my weaknesses, the kind of person I am," he added.

"The kind of person I am" was eloquently defended during the campaign by the brilliant black congressman from Atlanta, Andrew Young, in an angry letter to the editor of the newspaper *Village Voice* in New York City after the paper had aimed a rough attack at Carter.

"Carter is one of the finest products of the most misunderstood region of our nation," he wrote. "You are probably right in questioning Jimmy's doctrinaire liberalism, but progressive politics in 1976 must be based on a tough mind, and a tender heart and a loving, sensitive spirit."

12

WHAT TO EXPECT

He expects the best possible work. If he doesn't get it, he gets rid of you.

–A Carter aide

If Jimmy Carter makes it to the White House, the country is in for some surprises. The very first is likely to be the realization that this smiling, friendly, easygoing man from the Deep South is, in truth, a tough, impatient executive who demands, and gets, both hard work and excellence from those who work for him. That is the picture you get when you talk to his longtime aides, when you can catch them sitting still long enough to talk.

This is not to say that Carter's friendliness is a political "put-on" or that the smile is artificial. Those deep smile wrinkles could only be created by a lifetime habit. The point is that there are two Jimmy Carters—both of them the real thing. And when you vote for one, you get both. So it seems proper to shed some light on the one the public doesn't know.

To those who work with him, it's not "Jimmy," it's "the

governor." They speak of him with deference. When he takes off his campaigning hat and puts on his executive hat, they say, he becomes a no-nonsense combination of idea man, reformer and a boss who wants action—now!

He has a tendency to talk fast, his friends and staffers say, because he thinks fast, and because he doesn't like to waste time. "The governor" abhors staff conferences. He prefers to do his conferring by telephone. It's quicker that way, and easier to terminate by simply hanging up. The only time he loses his accustomed poise, they say, is when he gets behind schedule. It's then that the bystander gets a glimpse of "the governor" in action, giving sharp orders, with quick gestures. Things have got to move ahead on time, or the private Jimmy Carter gets very unhappy.

The governor is constantly in what one aide described as "a learning state of mind." He's always ready to examine new ideas, but if you've got a new idea, don't just try to talk it over with him informally. Boil it down to a brief memo. If he likes it, then he'll talk it over. If he approves the new idea, he'll embrace it with a total commitment. That, according to his staff, is the way he is with everything he considers worth doing.

Carter's work habits, his demand for excellence and his distaste for wasting time hark back to the days when he was in the navy and an assistant to the then-Captain Hyman Rickover, father of the nuclear submarine fleet, and who later became an admiral. Rickover is notorious for being the toughest boss in the navy. Carter, it is said, is one of the few people the admiral has some kind words for.

When you talk to Jimmy Carter he looks straight in your eyes, and there's no mistaking that he is listening. When he answers you know he has been listening. There are almost always questions.

The Carter mind is orderly. If the question at issue is complicated, the answer is likely to be laid out in points one, two, three, etc.

Gerald Rafshoon, an Atlanta friend and Carter's long-time campaign advertising director, pictured the governor as a "demanding boss who readily delegates authority to staff members who have his confidence.

"He doesn't get involved in details or try to do your work for you," said Rafshoon. "He expects the best possible work. If he doesn't get it, he gets rid of you."

Carter rarely loses his temper, according to those close to him. Instead, when something goes wrong, he becomes cold and methodical.

As a campaigner, Carter impressed the groups he met as intelligent, quick and deeply informed. Though he didn't talk much about the issues, he came through with occasional flashes that showed he had a good grasp of most of them. He confessed, frankly to his supporters that "I've got a lot to learn, and I know it, but I think I will learn fast from good friends like you."

Carter is well-read, and his interests range far afield from politics. Up to the start of the campaign his favorite authors were said to be William Faulkner, James Agee and Dylan Thomas. Lately, said members of his family, he has concentrated on politics, philosophy, history, taxation policy and foreign affairs.

On the campaign trail, reporters dubbed him "the first bionic candidate." One reporter wrote that Carter "is a clockwork candidate, who gets up earlier, turns in later, burns more jet fuel, exhausts more shoe leather, squeezes more hands, eyeballs more eyeballs, grins more grins and believes more serenely in himself than anybody else in the Democratic class of '76."

Once, reporters said, in the heat of campaigning in Mississippi he shook the hand of a department store mannequin. He covered his mistake by quipping to an aide: "Better give her a brochure, too."

There isn't much humor in his make-up, but he is, on the other hand, a pleasant conversationalist. He doesn't hire any professional joke writers, and he doesn't tell jokes, as such. Now and then he stumbles on to something that is funny in a low-key way. And if it gets a good laugh, he'll use it over and over again.

Here's one example:

"I don't claim to be the man best qualified to be president of the United States," he told an audience. "There are, right here in this room, people better qualified to be president than I am," he added, sober faced. Then, with the hint of a twinkle in his eye, he said, as a sort of afterthought: "And I want to thank you for not running this year. I've already got competition enough."

He also stirred laughter—and made a good impression—when, asked what his policy toward the Spanish-speaking people would be, he answered in Spanish.

Carter's habit of single-minded concentration and his impatience with time-wasters have invariably raised questions about his ability to get along with Congress and the slow-moving Washington bureaucracy. Is he going to be as stubborn in the Oval Office as he was in the governor's mansion in Georgia? There Carter's inner qualities of iron will and immovable adherence to moral principles proved to be something of a handicap.

Some people in the Carter camp have thought their man might have difficulty in compromising with Congress. He just might—in his own words—"prefer to go down in flames," they feared. But what they really feared most was that a succession of "down-in-flames" incidents could lead to acute disillusionment and frustration and cripple the Carter administration.

His aides believed that Carter would hold more press conferences than either Presidents Ford or Nixon. Because of the revolutionary nature of Carter's plans to streamline the federal government it would seem logical to expect him to have a stormy relationship with Congress. And one way to defeat a reluctant Congress is to carry the debate to the people by way of televised presidential press conferences. So the increased number of press conferences would not necessarily indicate that President Carter would have any greater love for the press than did President Ford or even President Nixon. But all indications were that he might be more clever in his use of the press—and the press conference—than either of his predecessors.

What kind of a president would Carter be, then?

He was asked this question at least once, in a press interview, and he answered it this way: "Most of my attitude toward government is very aggressive. I wouldn't be a quiescent or a timid president."

In the opinion of Governor Carter, Harry Truman was the best president of modern times—"he exemplified the kind of administration I would like to have."

He said he admired Truman's "honesty, his vision in foreign policy and his closeness with the American people." On the other hand, he also admired John F. Kennedy as "a much more inspirational president than Mr. Truman." Lyndon Johnson's "deep concern for the poor and the weak, and his skill in pushing legislation through Congress," also received high marks from Mr. Carter. He will try, he said, to emulate the strong points of all three of these Democratic leaders of the immediate past. Carter, at other times, expressed admiration for Winston Churchill, whom he considered to have been "the pre-eminent leader of our time."

One of the more cynical reporters who accompanied Carter in mid-campaign and who took note of the heroes he most admires, was moved to comment that: "Obviously, no single mortal can combine all these qualities. But I wonder if Jimmy Carter knows that? He'll probably give it a try, anyway."

As for the government itself, there should be both good news and bad news for the bureaucrats under President Carter. First, the good news: They will not become unemployed. And the bad news: They will likely get new jobs that will demand hard work and excellence. Carter often quotes the ancient biblical proverb, "He also that is slothful in his work is brother to him that destroys" (Proverbs 18:9).

It was the "sinful waste" in Washington that gave Carter the idea that he ought to try for the presidency. He wanted the people of the country to get from Washington the full measure of what they were paying for. It is noteworthy that he did not make promises to spend less money. He did not deny that he might even spend more, for Carter is an activist and a "doer."

In the eighteen months before the election he preached often against the "bloated" state of the bureaucracy, the "wasteful" spending, the "costly errors" that poured billions into the wrong hands, the "unmanageable" programs, especially in the area of welfare and the excessive government secrecy.

His aim in trying for the White House job is to preside over the complete reorganization of the government, from top to bottom. With God's help, he said, he will try to create a government that is efficient and economical and at the same time, "open, honest and compassionate."

He estimated that the reorganization would take about a year. "It will require the combined wisdom of the president and his staff, the Congress and professional civil servants, as well as the talents and advice of business, labor, consumer groups and the legal community," he said.

"I did it in Georgia, and not only did we save a lot of money and make it more efficient and economical, but we opened up government so that people could understand it and control it."

As for the federal employees themselves, Carter said, "I see a tremendous amount of frustration among the Civil Service employees of the federal government—particularly their leaders—in their inability to let their personal careers be realized in fruitful service. They're good people. The people in government yearn for a chance to throw off the burden of red tape, confusion, duplication, political manipulation and lack of goals and freedom."

Carter believes that the government has a proper role as a solver of social problems, but that it should be careful not to take away the incentive for people to solve their own problems. He explained that this did not mean his administration would do less for the people, or spend less in doing it, but that it would try to do more, for the same amount of money.

Another change would be in the source of tax money. Much of the tax burden would be removed from real estate (homes) and sales taxes, because these sources of revenue hit the poor much harder than they hit the rich. He believes that the federal income tax is the fairest tax of all.

He said he would create a completely new national welfare system, consolidating most of the one hundred or more different welfare plans into one or two based on a single nationwide payment in money for those in need of it, the payment to be varied only according to variations in the cost of living. Most of the nation's two million social workers, who now concentrate on paper work, would be transferred to jobs where they would perform direct services for the ill, the aged and the poor, under his program.

Carter proposed, in the field of the federal revenue sharing, to by-pass the state governments and send the money directly to the cities and towns. He would also ask Congress to alter the law so revenue-sharing funds might be used for schools and day-care and nursery centers for children of working mothers.

At a meeting of mayors in New York City at the height of the campaign in the spring, Carter said, "I've been hearing about comprehensive health care, welfare reform and tax reform ever since I was a youngster, and the programs never quite get passed. That's one reason I want to be president, so that when I'm in the White House I can propose to the Congress bold programs to revise these efforts for social care."

When he introduced an outline of a proposed national health program, to be paid for by contributions from employees and employers, and partly from the general treasury, he said he was advised that much of the federal treasury's part of the financing could be taken from the savings made possible by his reorganization of the structure of the federal government.

Carter had his eye on what he called the 1,900 "overlapping agencies" in Washington. He said his plan was to reduce them to about two hundred efficient, streamlined units. But he gave the voters fair warning not to expect a big reduction in the cost of what the federal government did for them. "A reduction in the bureaucracy doesn't necessarily mean a total reduction in personnel," he said. "But it does mean a shifting of personnel from useless paper work to more and better services in health, education, welfare, environmental protection and similar services."

In private conferences with business leaders he voiced the view that domestically the United States should give top priority to cutting unemployment, and take its chances with inflation. "When we get down to four to four-and-a-half percent unemployment, we won't have to worry about inflation," he said.

Unlike most Democrats in Congress, Carter thinks the big push for more jobs should start in private industry. He gave tentative approval, however, to the Humphrey-Hawkins full-employment bill "with amendments." The bill aims at what he once said is an unrealistic jobless rate of only three percent and he feared it would bring back double-digit inflation. He didn't say exactly what he meant by "with amendments" but he told campaign audiences he thought four percent unemployment combined with four percent inflation "we could live with."

To increase private jobs, Carter suggested federal aid to emerging new industries like solar energy and to services that called for large numbers of employees, like day-care centers, nursing homes and hospitals. He would also take away the corporation tax breaks that made it possible for American companies to locate plants outside the United States at a savings, leaving American workers with fewer jobs. He also suggested a revolutionary idea for the government to share the costs of a shorter work week (which would require more workers to do the same amount of work). This, he explained, would be done in industries that would otherwise lay off part of their work force.

On defense matters, the candidate believes the United States Navy is the most important arm of the defense establishment in peacetime, because ability to control the seas makes possible the execution of a peaceful and successful foreign policy. This view likely reflects his experience in the navy, especially under Rickover.

He is convinced, now, that the navy is dropping behind the Soviet navy, and needs a sizeable and immediate ship-building program. This could be financed, he suggested, by cutting five to eight billion dollars of waste out of the Pentagon budget, closing some overseas bases, and possibly delaying or scrapping the B-1 bomber.

In the foreign policy area, he seemed to suggest a good-neighbor sort of idealism, combined with a pragmatic toughness in dealing with foreign troubles.

He specifically laid out a "Carter Doctrine," which essentially voiced a determination never again to get involved militarily in the internal affairs of another nation unless United States security was directly threatened. It would not rule out involvement in South Korea if that country were attacked by North Korea, he said, "because we are already involved there."

"We have a commitment made by the Congress, the president, the people, and the United Nations," he added.

"I would prefer to withdraw all of our troops and land forces from South Korea over a period of years—three, four years, whatever. But, obviously, we're already committed in Japan. And we're already committed in Germany.

His doctrine, he said, would have applied to South Vietnam. And, he said, "It would apply, in recent months, to the attempt in Angola. It would apply, possibly, in the future, in a place like Rhodesia."

"I just wouldn't do it [become involved]," he said. "The American people don't need it. We don't have to show that we're strong. We are strong. And I just wouldn't get involved militarily."

Carter indicated that he doubted the federal budget could be balanced before 1980. An aide said the candidate was "a Keynesian on the budget." He would not want mandatory wage and price controls but thought the president should have stand-by authority to slap controls on industries or unions that got too greedy. He would use the presidential power of persuasion before resorting to the controls.

The candidate said he would "do all I can to encourage lower interest rates, but I would not meddle with the independent Federal Reserve Board."

The Carter camp talked of a tax revision that would involve the elimination of nearly all deductions, the tax treatment of all kinds of income exactly the same as wages, interest, capital gains—and a ban on taxing any income more than once. Double-taxation of company profits has been a sore point with stockholders for many years.

The overall aim of his tax reform, Carter said, would be to simplify greatly the tax system (and the job of making returns) and also to extract an increasing percentage as the amount of an individual's income rises. He believes the present tax system is "an absolute disgrace to the human race. It taxes the workers' wages more heavily than the millionaire's stock profits, and lets a businessman write off a fifty-dollar lunch, while a truck-driver can't deduct his lunch-counter sandwich."

The Democratic candidate has been sharply criticized for suggesting that some of the politically popular tax breaks—like the deductions for home mortgage-interest payments—ought to be ended along with the other more unpopular ones, such as corporate write-offs. But despite the fear that this strikes the hearts of new homeowners, he stood firm insisting that mortgage-interest deductions benefit the rich more than the poor. He estimated that ten billion dollars in tax revenue was being lost through this loophole. But he explained that the mortgage deduction would be eliminated only as part of the overall tax reform, and not as a tax change by itself.

But he would not hoard additional revenue gained under his plan or fritter it away on projects unrelated to housing. He proposed instead to use it to finance a program of federal aid to housing for lower and medium income people. He thought such a massive program—a ten billion dollar one—would go far toward bringing prosperity back to the housing industry and creating a wave of new jobs, not only in construction, but also in the industries that make furniture, fixtures, electrical apparatus, rugs, and everything else that goes into a home once it is built.

When President Truman was battling his hardest near the close of the tough campaign of 1948, the campaign in which he only narrowly avoided defeat by Thomas E. Dewey, one of his friends took him aside to offer a word of advice.

"Look, Mr. President," he began, "some of us think you may be hammering a bit too hard. Those things you're saying—they are embarrassing a lot of people. They're cheering you out there, but you're making some powerful enemies along with it. . . ."

The president shook his head, a little impatiently, and interrupted, "People say I'm giving them hell, but it's only the truth that I'm giving them. And they think the truth is hell."

That, in essence, is the message and the warning that Carter tried to get across in 1976. His message, and his warning boiled down to this: "Truth must be told, it must be known, or—as in the case of Watergate—truth, withheld in secrecy, can be hell in a very literal sense when it is finally revealed."

For years, Carter has studied intensively and prayed about the failures and successes of government. The key to his philosophy of government is found in a simple two-line verse in the Gospel according to John, chapter 8, verse 32: "And ye shall know the truth, and the truth shall make you free." That says it all.

As president, Mr. Carter promised he will run an "open" administration. What he means by that was described in the four lessons he says he learned from Watergate:

1. "We must strip away secrecy from government in every possible way; open up to the people the deliberations of the executive and legislative branches of government."

2. "Give the people access to our government in other ways: For example, cabinet members should go before joint sessions of Congress to be examined and questioned about foreign affairs, defense, agriculture and so forth."

3. "I will never get militarily involved in the internal affairs of another country, unless our own security is directly threatened."

4. "We must make the government mechanism work. It's an ineffective, bloated, confused, unmanageable bureaucracy now. And it hurts our people worse than anything I can think of, almost, even more than a lack of integrity in government. Competence is a missing element."

"Trust in government must be restored," Carter said. "But the only way to restore the trust of the American people in their government is for the government to be trustworthy."

The former governor of Georgia thought that the reason why he attracted such broad support in the presidential campaign was that he had always tried to carry out his promises to help those who could not help themselves.

"The ones who cling to me as a friend," he said, "are the ones who, throughout their whole lives, have been deprived of an opportunity to make decisions about their own lives.

"I saw clearly, as governor of Georgia—I see clearly now as a prospective or possible president—that in almost every instance, the people who make decisions in government that affect human things, very seldom are the ones who suffer when their decisions are wrong.

"The people who carved out a disgraceful, wasteful, confused, overlapping welfare system—their families never have to draw welfare.

"The people who carved out a disgraceful tax system—they don't ever get hurt because they're cared for when the tax laws are written.

"The criminal justice system—we pride ourselves in having a good, fair criminal justice system. It's not fair. Wealth is a major factor in whether or not you get justice.

"I think one of the major responsibilities I have, as a leader and as a potential leader, is to try to establish justice."

The governor explained that he did not mean strictly justice as obtained in the courts, but justice "in a broad gamut of things: in international affairs, peace, equality, racial discrimination and injustice, and in the nation's tax programs. . . ."

The purpose of government, said Carter, is "to provide for things that we can't provide ourselves." He identified those things this way:

"To provide legitimate services to our people.

"To preserve the peace.

"To provide a mechanism by which the people's character can be expressed in international affairs.

". . . to alleviate inequities."

And the president who heads such a government, what is his role and his purpose? Carter told repeatedly of his search for God's guidance on this question and his intensive study of the programs, the mistakes and the successes of those who had held the highest office. This is his overall answer to the search for clues to a successful presidency:

First of all, for the good of the country and the people, the president must work effectively with Congress.

"The president must be strong and aggressive, innovative and sensitive, working with a Congress that's strong, independent, in harmony, with mutual respect, and in the open, with a minimum of secrecy."

"I don't think that Congress is capable of leadership.

"That's no reflection on Congress. You can't find 535 people leading a nation.

"I don't think the founding fathers ever thought that Congress would lead this country.

"There's only one person in this nation who can speak with a clear voice for the American people.

"There's only one person who can set the standard of ethics and morality and excellence and greatness, or who can call on the American people to make a sacrifice—and explain the purpose of the sacrifice. . . .

"There's only one person who can answer the difficult questions and propose and carry out bold reforms, or provide for a defense posture that will make us feel secure, and a foreign policy that makes us proud once again.

"That's the president.

"In the absence of that leadership, there is no leadership, and the country drifts.

"So—a strong president? Yes.

"An autocratic or imperial president? No."

13

'I HAVE A VISION'

My critics don't want to stop Car-
ter. They want to stop the reforms I
am committed to. They want to
stop the people of this country
from regaining control of their
government.

–Jimmy Carter

Fifteen hundred husky, big-fisted labor union officials slumped in their chairs, their sleeves rolled up and their collars open while Idaho's Senator Frank Church, in his best oratorical tones, told them why he ought to be elected president of the United States. They had been sitting there, in Cincinnati's public auditorium, for three days, since the start of the 1976 convention of the Ohio State AFL-CIO. Obviously, to most of them it seemed longer. They rested their arms on the long, covered tables that divided the rows of convention delegates. Some were doodling on the tablecloths. Others drummed on the tables with their fingers. As the senator boomed at them through the loudspeakers there was an audible undertone of mumbled conversations. They had been hearing speeches of one kind or another for nearly seventy-two hours. They looked like a crowd that just couldn't absorb another word.

But the senator is an old hand at waking up tired audiences. And he made a beautiful effort. Point by point he built his case. With each step toward the climax his voice rose. And when he finally hammered home a major point it resounded through the hall. And then there was a pause for approval, as he leaned over to check his outline for the next point. It was a beautifully timed performance. And the unionists, tired as they were, responded in all the right places.

As the senator wound it up with a pitch for the union vote, he got a standing ovation—maybe for forty-five seconds to a minute. And as he made his way through the crowd he accepted friendly slaps on the back, complimentary comments on his talk and some crushing handshakes. His campaign aides smiled and nodded happily to each other. And then the crowd slumped back into the springy, plastic seats with a collective sigh to hear the final political speech of the meeting.

The speaker: Jimmy Carter, a man few of them had ever seen in the flesh or heard before.

There was a polite round of applause, and most of the convention crowd rose to its feet as the former Georgia governor, dressed in a light blue-gray summer-weight suit, a light blue shirt and a striped tie to match, stepped up onto the platform.

It was one of the labor union men who introduced him—a member of a delegation pledged to vote for Carter. Like most Carter speeches, it was a low-key introduction:

"This is a man who knows what it is to be poor. He knows what it is to work with his hands. He knows what it means to fail. He has known great success—in his business life, his personal life and in politics. Most of all he knows how to do the job he is asking for. He proved this by his performance as the governor of Georgia. And he has proved that he knows how to get the job he is asking for. He is now the front-runner among all the candidates for the Democratic nomination; the man who will be the next president of the United States: Jimmy Carter!"

There was a ripple of applause from the tired delegates, and here and there a cluster rose to its feet to applaud. Then there was silence.

Many of the delegates who had slumped and mumbled before, leaned forward in their chairs, with elbows on the table in front of them. You could sense a change of attitude. You could almost hear the collective mind telling them: "This may be something new. Let's hear what he has to say."

To begin with, the tone of the speech was radically different from the one Senator Church had just delivered.

"I talked with George Meany in Washington the other day," Carter began, in a low, conversational tone. "And he agreed with me that nothing would help the economy of this country more than a revival of the housing industry."

Without waiting for a sign of audience approval, he went on:

"The banks have the money to lend. There are millions of Americans who would borrow the money if there were houses to buy. There are millions of jobless building workers who are ready to go to work and build houses. . . ."

Still talking in a man-to-man tone, as if in private conversation with each one of the fifteen hundred, Carter turned to foreign affairs. "We must be friendly with the Russian people," he said, "but tougher in negotiations with their government. The American and Russian peoples can insure peace in the world only by getting to know each other better. They are both good peoples."

But the Ford and Nixon administrations, he charged, have been outmaneuvered by the Russians every time they get together for negotiations. "We sold our wheat too cheaply. So our farmers lost money. And the Russians turned around and sold it to some of our overseas customers at a profit that should have gone into American pockets."

The U.S. was outmaneuvered at Vladivostok, he said, and is being outmaneuvered in the SALT talks.

To the reporters who were traveling with him, this was all "old stuff." Not a pen or pencil was moving. The cassette tape recorders that most of them carry were left lying idle.

Then, suddenly, the whole tone of the speech changed. He had finished laying out his programs and his policies for inspection. And, all of a sudden, he was a fighting candidate, warning them that the "forces that want things to stay as they are" were plotting, not against Carter, but against the programs that Carter promised for the future of America.

The reporters began to sit up and reach for their notebooks. Cassette recorders were turned on. And the union leaders, sensing the turn, moved up in their chairs and leaned forward.

"We have seen this campaign come full circle now, from 'Jimmy Who?' to 'Stop Carter,' " the candidate declared. "The people who ignored me then are opposing me now. But mine is still the same campaign it was a year ago when I traveled alone and spoke in living rooms and meeting halls in Iowa and Florida and New Hampshire and every other state.

"The potential for a revival is there. All that is needed is ready and waiting. But the Republican administration is doing nothing to bring these things together so the construction industry can be revived. This is a job the government has to do."

Speaking without notes or text, Carter again continued, ignoring a few who tried to start a wave of applause.

"I know the importance of public housing, too," he said. "When I got out of the navy, with a wife and small children, I had no place to live. I had no money, except some war bonds. So we moved into a public housing project. My rent was twenty-eight dollars a month.

"When I was growing up, there was no running water in our home. There was no inside toilet. I knew what it was to work in the fields, the hardest kind of work. . . ."

By this time, his audience was listening. There was no undertone of conversation. There was no coughing, no head-scratching, no shuffling of feet. And nobody was walking out on this last of the political speeches.

He told them that he favored the Humphrey-Hawkins Bill, which would provide publicly financed jobs to bring unemployment down to three percent, but he emphasized that he came to support it only after it was amended. And the amendment that removed his opposition was one that put primary emphasis on creating jobs in private industry—jobs that can be created, he said, by government aid to newly developing industries; industries like solar heating, production of new kinds of energy.

Only as a last resort, he said, should the government create public service jobs to give work to those still unemployed.

There was no applause, but there was also no overt sign of disapproval. They were still listening—intently.

"My critics don't want to stop Carter. They want to stop the reforms I am committed to. They want to stop the people of this country from regaining control of their government. They want to preserve the status quo, to preserve politics as usual, to maintain at all costs their own entrenched, unresponsive, bankrupt, irresponsible political power."

This was a new Carter. One who had not, in two years of campaigning for the presidency, been displayed thus publicly. It was a Carter who sensed the danger in the stale odors of the smoke-filled rooms. A Carter who, with more than a thousand delegates pledged to his candidacy, made it clear that he could see the plots to prevent his nomination, and was determined to foil them.

It was the same Carter who—only two days before—had warned gently, but unsmilingly, that "if I should not get the nomination, the people of the South might think it was because I come from the South."

In that case, he said, the people of the South might feel some resentment toward the Democratic party. He hastily added that he, personally, would support the Democratic nominee, even if it turned out to be somebody else. And he pledged that he would "try" to convince the people of the South that they had not been robbed of their first chance at the presidency in more than one hundred years. But his voice did not carry conviction that this could be done. To his listeners, at a press conference in Trenton, New Jersey, his words were a reminder that the Democratic party had never in modern times won a presidential election without strong support from the South.

Having laid this plain warning before his Cincinnati labor convention audience, candidate Carter switched again to his vision of America in years ahead—a vision portrayed in words that sounded like an acceptance speech that might have been written by John F. Kennedy, or Martin Luther King, Jr., or both:

"I am running for president," he said, "because I have a vision of a new America, a different America, a better America, and it is not shared by those who are trying so hard to stop my campaign.

"I have a vision of an America that is, in Bob Dylan's phrase, busy being born, not dying.

"I see an America that is poised not only at the brink of a new century, but at the dawn of a new era of responsive, responsible government.

"I see an America that has turned her back on scandals and corruption and official cynicism and finally demanded a government that deserves the trust and respect of her people.

"I see an America with a tax system that is responsive to its people, and with a system of justice that is even-handed to all.

"I see a government that does not spy on its citizens, but respects your dignity and your privacy and your right to be let alone.

"I see an America in which law and order is not a slogan, but a way of life, because our people have chosen to bind up our wounds and live in harmony.

"I see an America in which your child and my child and every child, regardless of its background, receives an education that will permit full development of talents and abilities.

"I see an America that has a job for every man and woman who wants to work.

"I see an America that will reconcile its need for new

energy sources with its need for clean air, clean water and an environment we can pass on with pride to our children and their children.

"I see an American foreign policy that is as consistent and generous as the American people and that can once again be a beacon for the hopes of the whole world.

"I see an America on the move again, united, its wounds healed, its head high; an America with pride in its past and faith in its future, moving into its third century with confidence and competence and compassion, an America that lives up to the nobility of its constitution and the decency of its people.

"I see an America with a president who does not govern by vetoes and negativism, but with vigor and vision and positive, affirmative, aggressive leadership.

"This is my vision of America.

"It is one that reflects the deepest feelings of millions of people who have supported me this year. It is from you that I take my strength and my hope and my courage as I carry forth my campaign toward its ultimate success."

Carter paused for just a moment, as if to go on. Then, breaking into a smile, he said: "Thank you. God bless you."

The audience in that vast hall—all fifteen hundred of them—rose to its feet and applauded. And this time the applause was not a formality. There was enthusiasm behind it.

Though the word had not been passed to these labor-convention delegates—always sensitive to the word that comes from the level just above—that labor would support this man, it was plain to visitors that many of them were impressed.

And in the back of some of their minds there might have been a recollection of a statement by George Meany, president of the AFL-CIO, after his talk with Carter in Washington. Meany had said, in effect, "I would have no trouble supporting Mr. Carter if he gets the nomination."

And there was the added remark made by one of the

Meany aides: "If Carter gets the nomination, we'll find more things about him to like than even his mother ever thought of."

Twenty-four hours after the Cincinnati labor convention speech, the Carter campaign plane landed in Akron, Ohio, the nation's rubber industrial capital. And there the United Rubber Workers Union invited him to hold his rally in their union hall. He did, and it drew a standing-room-only crowd.

There was none of the "get-tough" talk this time. It was a good-natured give-and-take of questions and answers, for the most part, with a repeat performance of his visions of America's future to wind it up. The tone was set by the very first question from the crowd:

"Who is your favorite vice president?" a voice from the rear shouted.

Carter smiled broadly and replied: "Harry Truman."

When the laughter subsided, he apologized for poking fun at the question. "I know what you mean," he said, "but I think it would be presumptuous of me to start naming vice presidents when I haven't even got a nomination yet."

Every reporter who travels with a presidential candidate wastes no time before asking for an exclusive interview. If you can catch him in the proper mood, there's nothing like a man-to-man talk with a presidential aspirant to bring out his true character. But when, as usual, you have thirty or forty newsmen in the entourage, you have a long wait, and you have to take your turn whenever it comes, and whatever the circumstances.

So it was that a veteran reporter's turn came as Carter left the Rubber Workers Hall in Akron to drive by motorcade, at the height of the rush hour, to the Akron airport. He was ushered into the back seat of the Carter limousine beside the candidate, and was told that his turn would end when they arrived at the airport, about twelve or fifteen minutes later.

They had met before, but the reporter thought he'd better start all over again. Carter had met many thousands since their last few words together.

"Governor," he began, "I represent the *National Courier*, a Christian newspaper. I am a Republican, and I have never voted for a Democrat in my life. But we are both Christians and that, I think, sort of makes us members of the same party. I think there are millions of other Christians in the country who would like to know exactly what kind of a Christian you are. So if you don't mind, I'm going to ask you some questions about your spiritual life."

Carter smiled and gave a quick nod and said, "Sure. Go ahead."

Speaking slowly and thoughtfully he told of his conviction that the American people deserve a better, more honest, more compassionate and efficient government, and of his gradual realization that he himself might be the man to create such a government.

As his motorcade sped through rush-hour traffic he told of the support he had received from committed Christians all over the country. He dipped, also, into his past. He told of his defeat for the Georgia governorship and his feelings of deep depression, and his spiritual revival with the advice and counsel of his sister, Ruth Stapleton.

It was not until the motorcade arrived at the gates of the airport that they began to talk of Carter's two one-week missionary ventures into northern states, experiences which he said were among the most deeply moving of his spiritual life.

"Can you think of any particular thing that happened in that missionary period that most affected your life?" the reporter asked.

Carter turned and watched the passing traffic awhile before answering. Then, choosing his words carefully, he said:

"Well, it was primarily a sense of complete dependence on the Holy Spirit. You know, I had a feeling before I went that in my personal witnessing to families in which there was no Christian, that the intelligence that I could bring, and the forcefulness of my argument, and the eloquence of my discussion would be the major factor in convincing those people to accept Christ as their Savior."

The candidate's motorcade at this moment pulled up to the stairs of the campaign plane. A Secret Service man in the front seat got out, and started to open the rear door. Governor Carter motioned him away, pulled the door closed and continued:

"But I soon realized that when I thought I fumbled most, and when I thought I had failed, that was the very time when the people were convinced by the Holy Spirit, and I realized that it wasn't me, or my brilliance or my fervor that made the difference. It was something else—and that was the presence of the Holy Spirit. It was a major change. . . . Oh, I'm sorry. Here we are at the airplane," he said, reaching for the door again. "I've got to go."

As he stepped out the door and turned to shake hands, he added: "Good luck with the book."

The Carter plane taxied slowly out to the runway, and then began rolling, faster and faster, down past the old dirigible hangar and then off into the clouds toward Youngstown and the next rally. The reporter sat there clutching his cassette recorder as if it were a box of diamonds.

He felt then, and was even more certain later, that their brief encounter on the road to the Akron airport had produced a new piece of presidential history.

He had interviewed presidents and presidential candidates—both winners and losers—since the days of Franklin D. Roosevelt, over a period of thirty-six years, but never had any of them so candidly and openly bared his deepest spiritual experiences. He had never before heard a president or a candidate for that office talk about the Holy Spirit in his life.

As the empty motorcade headed back toward the city he tested the little recorder to make sure the conversation was all there. It was.